Mastering the E-6B Flight Computer

A Handbook For Student Pilots Who Need to Learn It

and

A Refresher For Licensed Pilots Who May Have (ahem) Forgotten It

This book is dedicated to the hundreds and hundreds (heck, thousands) of students who have survived my infamous "Navigation" lecture in ground school. I told them when they walked in the door that they would be able to do this, and before they left, they could. I'll tell you the same thing, and you'll be able to as well.

I also wish to extend my undying gratitude to my wife Ela M. Lugo, who read and reread this book, telling me "I don't understand this part!" and (dare I say it?) forcing me to rewrite it until she did. I never argue with my wife or my lawyer, and she is both.

Mike Arman, AGI

© 2006 Mike Arman
ISBN 0-933078-19-6

Table of Contents (What you're in for . . .)

Origins of the E-6B 3

Mastering the E-6B Flight Computer 4

What this book covers 5

Function 1: Temperature conversions 9

Function 2: Nautical to Statute (Knots to miles) 11

Function 3: Liters/US Gallons/Imp Gallons/Fuel Weight 14

Specific Gravity on the ARC-1 and CRP-1 Flight Computers 18

Function 4: Time, Speed, Distance 22

Function 5: Fuel Use 26

Function 6: Wind Triangles 29

Function 7: Density Altitude 36

Function 8: True Altitude 42

Function 9: True Air Speed, Compressibility, Mach number, other fables 46

Using the E-6B to plan a flight 48

Welcome to Metric-land 61

Metric-land to Grandma's Airport 69

Grandma's Airport to Home 75

Understanding Variation 78

Final Comments 80

Important! For best results, read, digest and understand ONE section at a time. Go slowly, some of this (a lot of this) is not intuitive. If you wait until the day before your written test or your flight test to start learning the E-6B, it is too late. Plan ahead and this will be easy. If something doesn't make sense, go back and read it again, slowly, perhaps out loud (where no one can hear you). If you absolutely, positively get totally and completely stuck, my e-mail address is Armanmik@earthlink.net.

For another copy of this book, let me know, or go to www.LearntheE6B.com. I also have a book called *Owning, Buying or Flying the Cessna 150/152*, details available at www.Cessna150book.com.

M. Arman Publishing
PO Box 785
Oak Hill, FL 32759

Origins of the E-6B

Philip Dalton joined the U.S. Navy Reserve in 1930, and earned his pilot's wings in 1931. Dalton was a recruiting officer's dream. Educated at Princeton, Cornell and Harvard, he was a research physicist and a consulting engineer. He quickly realized that most of the available pilot's aids were complicated, difficult to use, awkward, and simply not very good, so he decided to do something about it.

Dalton's first effort was the Model A, which was a circular slide rule which did time, speed and distance problems. The A was almost immediately superceded by the B, which was quickly, widely and enthusiastically adopted, usually with comments like "Why didn't I think of this?" and "Where can I get one of these?"

With time, speed and distance out of the way, Dalton then addressed the wind triangle problem. Pilots had been using "speed tables" to work out wind triangles, but like any awkward, difficult method of doing things, these speed tables were often ignored, and the pilots preferred to just get in the airplane and go, navigating by pilotage.

About a year after he developed the Model B, Dalton created the Mark VII, which also calculated the wind triangles. The Mark VII worked very well, but only up to about 160 mph. Airplanes were starting to go faster, and the only way to make the Mark VII work in faster airplanes was to make it longer. This made it awkward, and being made of 1930s plastic, very fragile.

Dalton's interim solution was the Model G, with an endless cloth belt which was moved by a knob through internal gearing. Even though the G was somewhat bulky and heavy, the U.S. Navy and the Royal Air Force used them anyway, usually strapped to the pilot's kneeboard. While it did work, Dalton was not satisfied with it and kept looking for a better solution.

Finally, in 1937, Dalton had the answer. Discarding the gearing, he made a rectangular, movable wind slide, and it worked perfectly. This was the E-6 model, and when the Model B time-speed-distance computer was grafted onto the back of the E-6, the result became the E-6B, which is in use to this very day.

Philip Dalton was unfortunately killed in an airplane accident in 1941, at the age of 38. His creation, the Dalton Dead-Reckoning E-6B Flight Computer, has been in constant use throughout the world for the past 65 years, and is still going strong. It is a living testament to his genius.

Mastering the E-6B Flight Computer

There is no surer sign that someone is a member of the Fraternity of Aviators than mastery of the E-6B Flight Computer.

Anyone can go buy a pair of sunglasses and a big wristwatch and then stand around assuming heroic poses to impress the masses. People on the "outside", passengers, friends, family, only see the aviator sunglasses and the dinner-plate sized wristwatch. They are (usually) suitably impressed - they know no better.

Aviators, however, know. Real aviators are not deceived by such "wanna-be" posers. Airplanes are not at all impressed by image either, and that dashing white scarf will not keep the engine running one second more when all the fuel is gone.

The E-6B is the tool and the badge of a genuine aviator. Properly used, the E-6B quickly and easily answers questions such as "How fast are we going?" and "How much fuel will we need?" and "What is the density altitude?" and "With an IAS of 150 knots and the wind from 220 at 30, how long will this trip take and what is the wind correction angle?"

Flight students in the 21st century often have a more difficult time with the E-6B than the people who learned to fly before the days of the pocket calculator. The E-6B doesn't light up, has no buttons, no batteries, isn't connected to the internet, and you have to go looking for the answer instead of having it presented to you on a display.

This is actually a significant advantage. The E-6B is never afflicted with a dead battery, sailed through Y2K with no compliance problems whatsoever, will function quite happily after being dropped, after having coffee or soda spilled on it, it works day or night, in sunshine or shade, hot or cold, it simply doesn't care.

It is also not subject to "garbage in, garbage out" like hand held calculators. If you mis-key something on a hand held unit, unless the answer is wildly wrong, you may not realize it. After all, a computer gave you these numbers, therefore they must be correct, right? With the old-fashioned, human-powered mechanical E-6B, errors become glaringly obvious. ("We're flying a Cessna 150 here, so I don't think our speed for the last leg was 865 knots . . . ")

Learning the E-6B is not at all difficult, and you can learn every function on it in less than a day. The major functions can be learned in a few hours. The E-6B is a tool, and it is a good one, well proven over time. Once you master it, it will serve you well indeed.

What this book covers

The intent of this book is to teach the uses and applications of the circular slide rule flight computer. There are three main types; the E-6B, which is used in the USA, and the almost-twin flight computers used in the UK and the metric world, known as the ARC-1 and the CRP-1.

Fortunately, all three work very much the same way, so mastery of one means you've got the others pretty well whipped, too.

Student pilots often fear these devices, and some experienced pilots have forgotten how they work, so this book can be used as an introduction, or as a refresher. Learning (or re-learning) how to use these flight computers is not difficult, and they are amazingly useful, which explains why they are still around. It also explains why they make you learn it as part of getting your license in the first place.

There are some other types of flight computers "out there", but your choice of the E-6B, the ARC-1 or the CRP-1 will do just about everything you need until you get your very own F-15. (When you do get your very own F-15, you'll also be able to hire someone to do this for you, but in the meantime, you have to do it yourself.)

E-6Bs can be had in several varieties. The least expensive version is made by Jeppesen-Sanderson, out of the finest aviation-grade cardboard. It costs about $11.00, and it is every bit as accurate and works every bit as well as any of the others, some of which are considerably more expensive, and some of which are breathtakingly more expensive. Best of all, the instructions are printed right on it, which is a stunningly obvious idea. Thank you, Eldon Jeppesen, where-ever you may be . . .

If you fear that being seen using a cardboard flight computer may detract from your desired image, aluminum E-6Bs are available from several sources. These tend to be more expensive, and are indeed a bit more rugged. In fact, they never wear out, and used ones can sometimes be found in aviation flea markets at fly-ins for under $5.00, which has to be one of the biggest bargains going in aviation.

One thing to watch is that after a few years, the wind index on the back tends to fall off because the glue dries out. You can re-install it with super-glue, but you need to be careful, because if you use too much super-glue you won't be able to turn the wheel any more. (The author prefers that you not ask how he knows this.)

You may notice that on many of the aluminum E-6Bs, there is a plastic ring on the upper right side of the center section. Believe it or not, this is for a lanyard to go around your neck, so you won't lose the E-6B over the side when you are doing aerobatics in your open cockpit biplane.

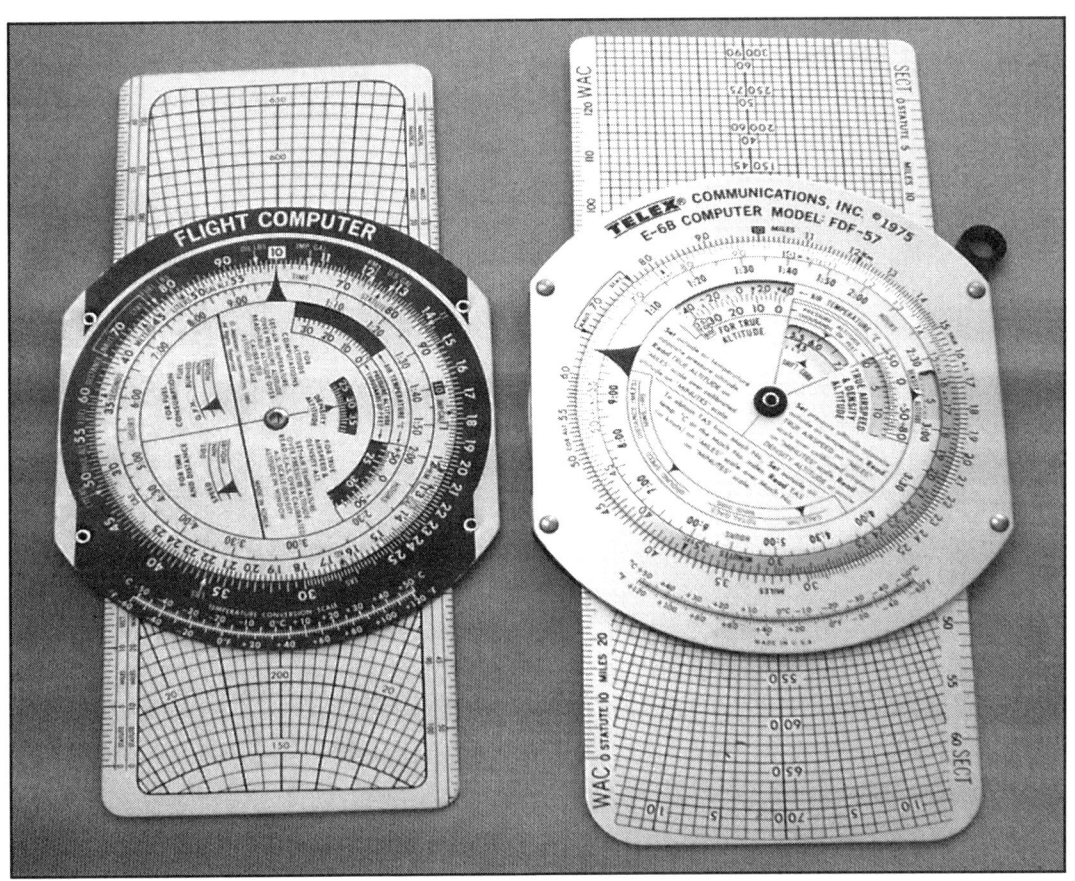

U.S. style E-6Bs. On the left is the cardboard Jeppesens model, on the right, an aluminum Telex.

When we cross to the other side of the pond, we find the UK-sourced ARC-1 and CRP-1. These are made of plastic, and in the author's opinion, are excessively expensive. The plastic is much more fragile than aluminum and much less forgiving than cardboard. Additionally, if you lay one of these down on the aircraft's glare shield in the hot summer sun, after a while your expensive plastic flight computer will strongly resemble the Salvador Dali clock and that makes it very difficult to turn the wheels. (Either that, or from now on you can only use it in the mountains.)

Both the ARC-1 and the CRP-1 figure fuel weights using specific gravity, and will give you an answer in pounds or kilograms (yes, you can choose) so, if you are flying in Euroland or any place else that uses the metric system, this is a great help. The ARC-1 and the CRP-1 can thus figure the weight of jet fuel, while the E-6B assumes you'll be flying a piston engine airplane, and that your fuel weighs six pounds per US gallon.

The UK twins don't have any instructions marked on them, so you'll have to remember what you're doing. Since the CAA doesn't seem to be particularly interested in making it easy for people to learn to fly, they will probably recommend that new versions of the ARC-1 and CRP-1 be marked only in Braille. ("Elementary, my good man. That's so you can use it in instrument conditions when you can't see.")

One nice thing about the UK twins is that they are color coded. Distance calculations on the CRP-1 are in red and fuel calculations are in blue, which matches the color of the fuel, 100LL. Just to keep things interesting, on the ARC-1, distances are blue and fuel is red. That matches the old 80-87 fuel, which is no longer available. The point is that if the colors in your calculation don't match, this will tell you something is wrong, since you are (hopefully) not trying to change kilometers to Imperial gallons.

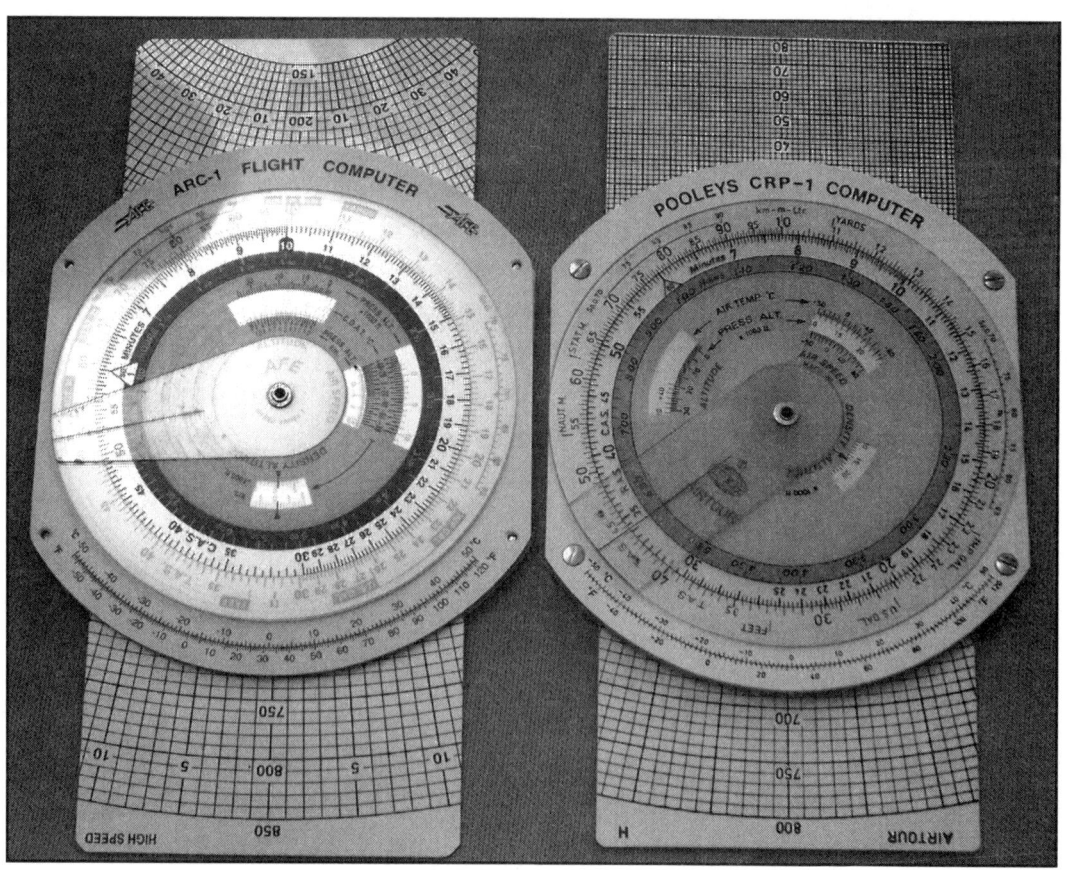

The U.K. twins. ARC-1 on the left, CRP-1 on the right.

Pooleys, who makes the CRP-1, also makes several other variations of it, including the CRP-5, which they tout as the "professional pilot's" version of the CRP-1. It is larger, and costs (a lot) more, but works the same way.

During the war, the C-Plath company in Hamburg made copies of the E-6B (known as the "Windrechner WR-2"), and so did the Japanese. They still make them, and you can buy German or Japanese produced E-6Bs at prices ranging from the merely astronomical ($120 for one of the German types) to the absolutely intergalactic (over $400 for one of the Japanese versions).

In the US, ASA and Telex (among others) make E-6Bs in various sizes. Aero Products of Los Angeles makes (or made) a version known as the CR-6, which works in a similar manner, but calculates wind triangles differently.

You may have noticed that sometimes this is called an E-6B and sometimes it is called an E6-B. After Dalton's patent ran out, several companies copied the original Dalton E-6B, and moved the hyphen in the name one digit to the right, from E-6B, to E6-B. A rose by any other name, you know . . .

In addition to the mechanical E-6B, there are some hand-held pocket calculator style E-6Bs available. These are battery operated, and in the opinion of this author are more for showing off to non-aviators ("Hey, look at me, I'm a PILOT!") than for real use. (Well, that's one vendor who won't be selling this book.) The major problem is of course the batteries. Computers invariably let you down when you need them the most. Further, using one of these on a check ride is not a good idea. Some check pilots will ask to examine this neat toy, admire it, and then put it in their pocket, saying "OK, it just failed. Continue the check ride." Guess what: If you didn't bring or can't use the "old fashioned" mechanical E-6B, you have just failed the check ride.

Finally, some "pilot's" wristwatches have partial E-6B scales built in or onto them. These are useful mostly if you normally fly carrying a microscope. The numbers are simply too small to be readable, and many of the functions you really do need are not even there. Besides, aviation is an expensive game, and by the time many people can afford it, their near vision isn't as good as it once was anyway. These wristwatches are actually designed to be SOLD TO pilots, as distinct from being USED BY pilots.

Ready?

Function 1: Temperature conversions

The easiest conversion of all - no moving parts!

Down at the bottom of the face of the wheel, there is a temperature conversion scale. It lets you convert from Fahrenheit to Centigrade and back. We'll need this because the outside air temperature gauge in your airplane is probably in Fahrenheit. Aviation weather reports and forecasts are now in Centigrade in the USA, and always were in much of the rest of the world.

Do we care about the temperature beyond deciding to wear a sweater or not? Yes, we do, and so does the airplane. Hot air is thin air and your airplane will not perform as well in hot air as it will in cold air. This concept is covered in the section on density altitude, and while it does make for some pretty dense reading (sorry), it is extremely important.

Since all the other calculations on the wheel use Centigrade, we get to take the reading off the airplane's thermometer (the OAT) or the thermometer at the FBO's front door, both of which are probably in Fahrenheit, and convert their readings to Centigrade.

All we do is find the number of degrees on either the C or F scales, and read across the center line to the other side, which gives us the equivalent in F or C. The hardest part here is squinting to read the tiny numbers.

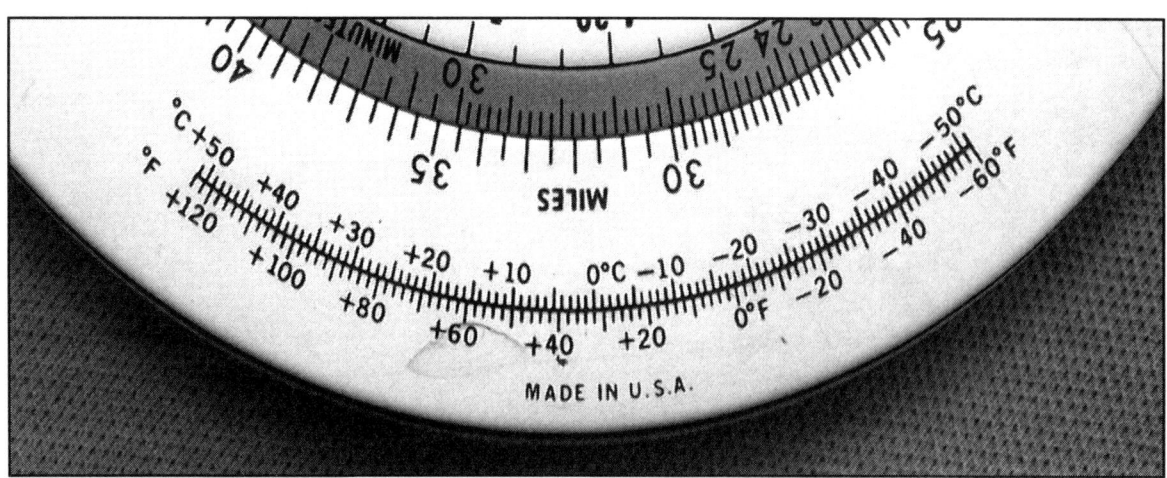

E-6B temperature conversion scale

ARC-1 temperature conversion scale.

Notice that the high temperatures are on the right and the low temperatures are on the left. This is exactly the reverse of the layout on the E-6B, but the usage is identical anyway. (They also claim we drive on the wrong side of the road.)

Function 2: Nautical to Statute (Knots to miles)

Nautical Miles (knots) to Statute Miles and reverse

Here's an easy one. Find the bracket on the outer scale around 70. This is used to convert Nautical Miles (Knots) to Statute Miles or reverse. All you need is the bracket on the outer scale and the speed, in either knots or miles per hour on the center (minutes) scale, and you can get the answer in miles per hour or knots. (Feel free to completely ignore everything else!)

"This airplane cruises at 110 KIAS, how many miles per hour is that?" Put 11 on the center scale under the Naut arrow, and read the answer on the center scale under the Stat arrow: 127 mph.

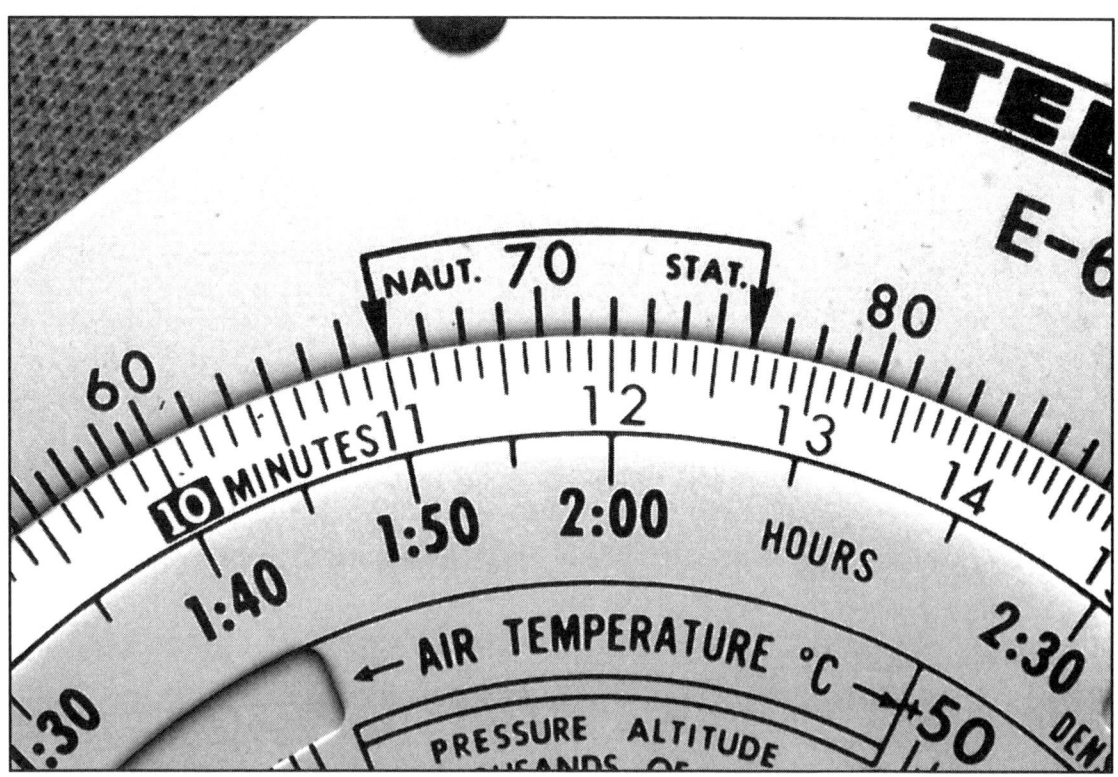

Alternatively, "This airplane is going 105 mph, what's that in Knots?" Place 105 on the center scale under Stat, read the answer on the center scale under the Naut arrow: 91 Knots.

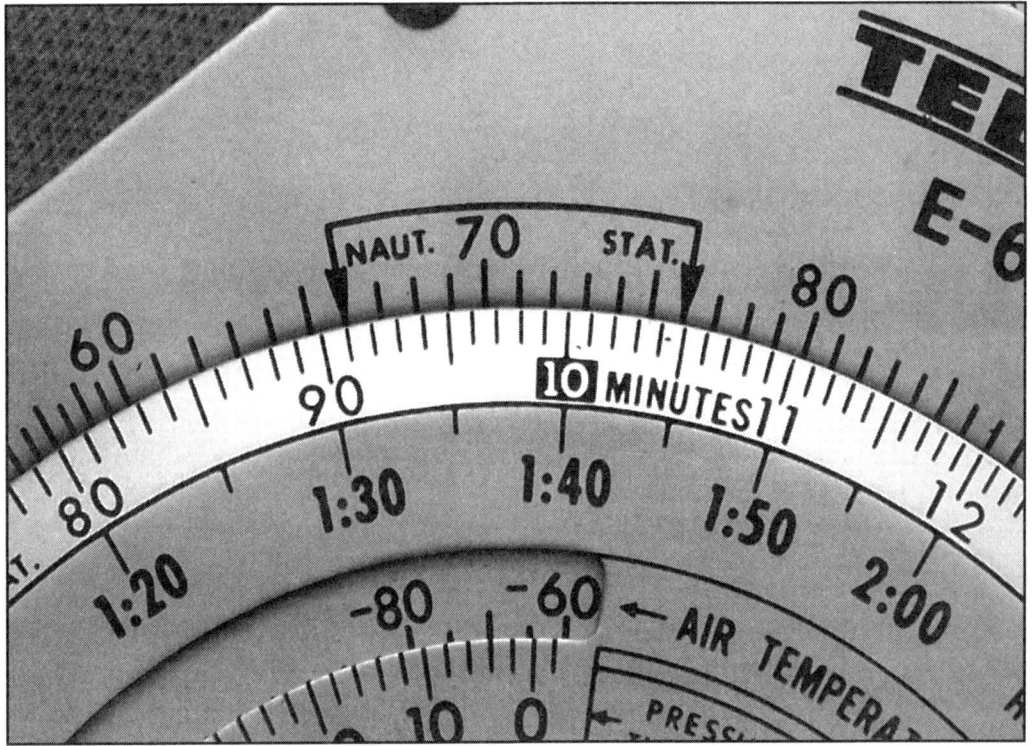

You would use these calculations in the following situations. Example one, your airplane has an air speed indicator calibrated in Knots, and your passenger asks you how fast we are going. "110 Knots" means absolutely nothing to most people - they have no idea how long a knot is, even if they have heard the term. Answering "127 miles per hour" gives them something they understand. As a side benefit, it also sounds more impressive. Since "127" is a bigger number than "110", we must be going faster!

Example two, your airplane has an ASI calibrated in miles per hour, but you are doing a flight plan, and everything else is in knots. Converting the airspeed to knots is far less work than converting everything else to miles, even if the resulting "speed" is "less" because 91 is less than 105, and therefore must be slower. If you want to feel better, however, look at the "KM" arrow just to the right of 12 on the outer scale, then read the number under it on the center scale - we are rocketing along at a blistering 169 Km/hr!

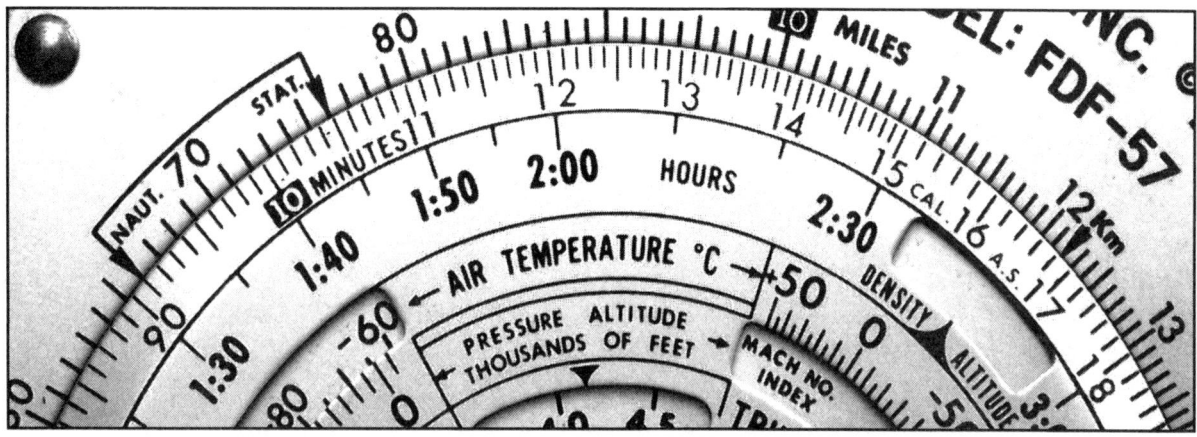

105 mph = 91 knots = 169 km/hr

You will notice that we used "11" for "110" and got "12.7" for "127".

We'll also need to use this conversion with weather reports. Aviation weather quotes the wind speed in knots, and your airplane may have an air speed indicator which reads in miles an hour. If your wind triangles (to be discussed later) are going to bear any relation to reality at all, you'll need to be working in the same unit of measure, either knots and knots or miles and miles.

As an easy example, a 30 knot wind is equal to 34.5 miles an hour.

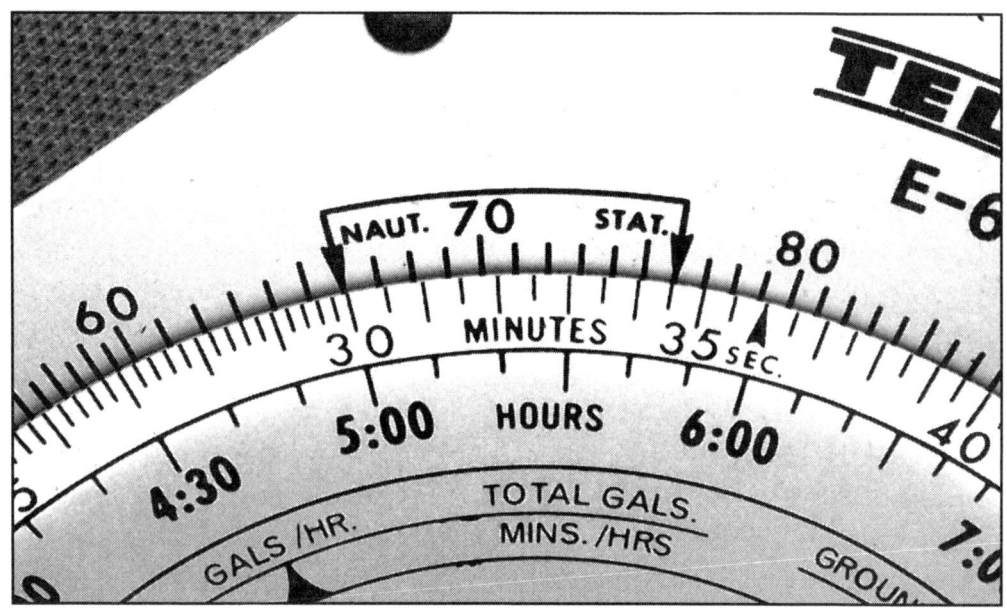

Function 3: Conversions - Liters/US Gallons/Imp Gallons/Fuel Weight

Fuel Weight and Quantity Conversions

How much fuel can we put in this aircraft? How much can our passengers weigh? The questions are simple; the answers are not.

The answers also have to be right because being wrong enough can be fatal, and it is fairly easy to be wrong. Unfortunately, we can't fill all the seats, all the baggage and all the fuel tanks and expect things to work out favorably.

Piston engine airplanes built in the USA have their load capacities stated in pounds, fuel capacities in gallons, and fuel consumption stated in gallons per hour.

Piston engine airplanes built in Europe have load capacities in kilograms, fuel capacities in liters, and fuel consumption stated in liters per hour.

Older British piston engine airplanes have load capacities in pounds, but may have fuel capacities in Imperial Gallons, so the fuel consumption is going to be in Imperial Gallons per hour as well.

Jet aircraft generally have their fuel capacities stated by weight, in pounds for US and British jets, and in kilograms for jets built in Euroland.

And of course, there are always exceptions since some designer, somewhere thinks he has a better idea and will state the fuel capacity in hogsheads or some other obscure and arcane measurement.

One of the top three reasons private pilots crash their airplanes is simply that they ran it out of fuel, whereupon the noise stopped. (The other two are "continued VFR into instrument conditions" and, believe it or not "hit something", and not necessarily the ground - at first - either!) This woeful performance happens even when our hero pilots are flying in their home territories and don't need to convert from pounds to kilograms to Imperial Gallons to hecto-deci-liters and so forth.

Now tell me what kind of results we can expect if we have an older British airplane with the fuel capacity stated in Imperial Gallons and we are buying fuel by the liter, we have a passenger who states his weight in kilograms, and we need to find the allowable fuel weight in pounds. Confused? I am.

Fortunately the E-6B and its twin British cousins, the ARC-1 and CRP-1, have the answers for us - as long as we know what we are doing. Here are the situations:

1) If we have an airplane of US origin and we are in the USA, we will be buying fuel by the gallon and calculating weights by the pound, just like we did back in ground school. (This assumes you are a US reader!) Example - we are flying a Cessna 172 in Florida.

2) If we have an airplane of US origin and we are overseas (almost anywhere), we are going to be buying fuel by the liter (converting back and forth to gallons) and again calculating weights by the pound. Example - we fly that Cessna 172 to Mexico or Canada. We may also have to calculate weights in and out of kilograms. If we take someone for a ride and ask their weight so we can calculate the weight and balance, their answer might be "80 kilograms", and you will not find "80 kilograms" unless you can find the conversion tables page in the Cessna Pilot's Operating Handbook. (80 kg = 175 pounds)

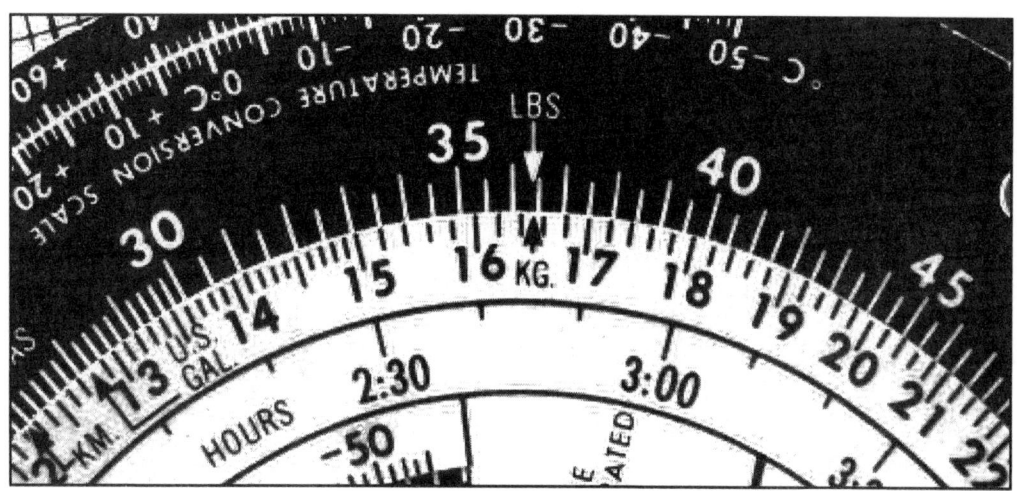

3) If we have an airplane of British origin, and we are not in the US, we are going to be buying fuel by the liter (converting back and forth to Imperial Gallons), and then calculating weights by the pound. Example - we are flying a Tiger Moth in England. Passengers who state their weights in kilograms (if we happen to be in Europe) will have to be converted to pounds as in example 2.

4) If we have an airplane of British origin, and we are in the USA, we are going to be buying fuel by the US gallon (converting back and forth to Imperial Gallons), and calculating weights by the pound. Example - we import the Tiger Moth to the USA and fly it in airshows.

5) If we have an airplane of European origin, and we are not in the USA, we are going to be buying fuel by the liter, and calculating weights by the kilogram. Example - we are flying a Yak 52. If we are in the UK, our passengers may state their weights in pounds (which we have to convert to kilograms) or even in "stones" (a "stone" is 14 pounds) - and you are NOT going to find that on any flight computer.

6) If we have an airplane of European origin, and we are in the USA, we are going to be buying fuel by the US gallon (and converting back and forth to liters), and calculating weights by the kilogram (and also converting back and forth to pounds). Example - we import the Yak 52 to the USA and fly it in the airshow after the Tiger Moth. Our passenger weights will also have to be converted to kilograms.

7) Just to keep things interesting, the older UK origin airplanes quote fuel capacity in Imperial gallons, newer ones in liters, and I am sure some UK aircraft, somewhere, uses US gallons. I have also seen the fuel capacity of Euro origin aircraft quoted in Imperial gallons, liters, and occasionally US gallons. When all else fails, read the Pilot's Operating Handbook.

Here's a graph which may help.

Location	USA	UK	Europe
US made aircraft	No conversions	Liters < > USG, Kg < > Lbs for fuel No conversion for cargo	Liters < > USG, Kg < > Lbs for fuel Kg < > Lbs for cargo
UK made aircraft	IG < > USG, No Lbs conversion	Liters < > IG, Kg < > Lbs for fuel Kg < > Lbs for cargo*	Liters < > IG, Kg < > Lbs for fuel Kg < > Lbs for cargo
Euro made aircraft	USG < > Liters, Lbs < > Kg for fuel Lbs < > Kg for cargo	No fuel conversion Lbs < > Kg for fuel Lbs < > Kg for cargo	No conversions

* means "maybe" or "sometimes"
Cargo refers to people and things, but not fuel.

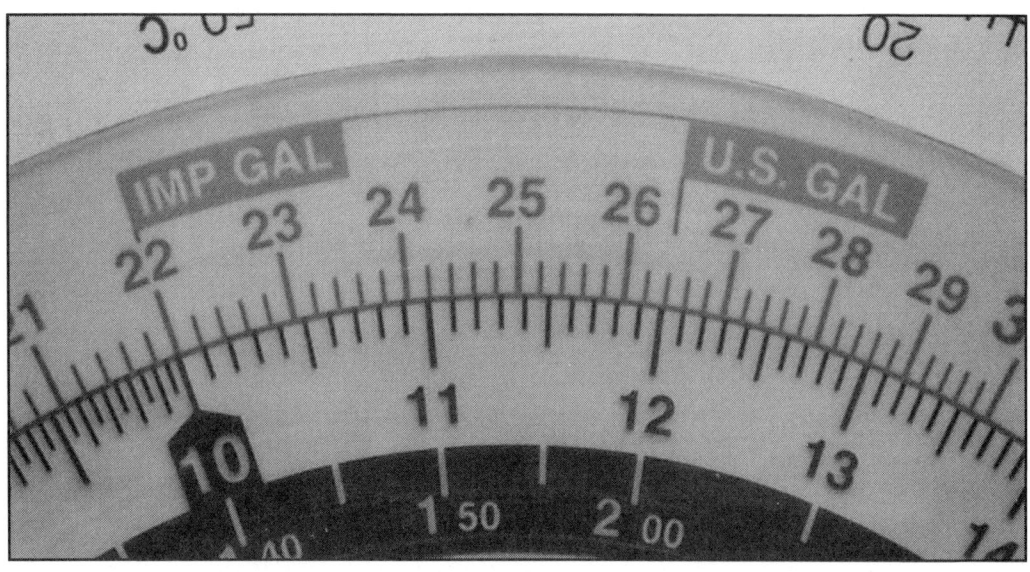

Conversion of 12 US gallons to 10 Imperial gallons

Notes about "stone". If you are really, really depraved, you might want to put an arrow at 26 on the center scale and mark it "stone". If you line up your "stone" arrow on the center scale with the "Lbs" arrow on the outer scale, you can convert back and forth to stone - the weight in pounds is on the outer scale above the value in stone on the center scale. Try it and see for yourself! (This only works on the E-6B, the ARC-1 and CPR-1 won't do this.)

If you are not only really, really depraved, but also a certified candidate for immediate heavy sedation, you can convert stone to kilograms by first converting it to pounds as above, then lining up the Lbs arrow on the outer scale with the "Kg" arrow on the center scale and taking the number of pounds on the outer scale and reading the Kg equivalent on the center scale. You should be aware that this much sedation will probably result in the loss of your medical and it is probably hard to operate the controls if you are wearing one of those padded white coats . . .

Anyway, as you can see, it is quite important that all our measurements be of the same "flavor", either all English (feet, pounds, gallons) or all Metric (meters, kilograms, liters).

Specific Gravity on the ARC-1 and CRP-1 Flight Computers

(A little side trip)

The UK style ARC-1 and CRP-1 flight computers figure fuel weight in a slightly different way than the US style E-6B. There is an extra step involved, and it relates to specific gravity.

Specific gravity is the metric way to compare the weights of different liquids to the weight of water. (It is also used on solids, but that does not concern us here.)

Specific gravity starts with a known item, and that is the weight of a liter of water. By definition, a liter of water weighs one kilogram, and by definition, the specific gravity of water is one. (Incidentally, that is at 4°C, the temperature at which water is most dense.) Other fluids may weigh more or less than the equal volume of water, and their specific gravity tells us how much more or less.

For instance, a fluid with a specific gravity of .6 will weigh 600 grams per liter, and a fluid with a specific gravity of 3 will weigh 3 kilograms per liter.

On the US style E-6B, gasoline is assumed to weigh six pounds per US gallon, and oil is assumed to weigh 7.5 pounds per US gallon. As it turns out, that isn't quite correct, but when we are dealing with small quantities, the error is small and doesn't really matter much.

Lets first look at automobile gasoline. In the US, the average specific gravity of auto gas is .734, and in the UK it is .737. This is a negligible difference. Avgas in the US has an average specific gravity of .716, and in the UK, it is .706. One gram per liter is again, not a heck of a lot.

Now lets look at it this way. We have an airplane with a fuel capacity of 100 US gallons, which is 378 liters. Fueled with UK avgas (sg .706), the fuel weight is 378 times .706 times 2.2 (answer in pounds) or 587.1 pounds. Now we fuel the airplane with UK car gas (sg .737), so the numbers are 378 times .737 times 2.2, or 612.9 pounds - a difference of 26 pounds.

Airplanes that can take 100 gallons of fuel (Bonanzas, Seminoles, etc.) are not likely to be bothered too terribly much by an extra 26 pounds, especially if it is fuel and will be burned off pretty soon anyway. True, the unexpected 26 pounds might put the airplane overgross, but on a 4,000 pound airplane, 26 pounds is about 5/8ths of one percent. In the real world, it doesn't make much practical difference. (Tell your passengers not to eat lunch before the flight, and that will take care of the extra 26 pounds.)

So here are some average specific gravities (according to the International Energy Agency, in a report from November 2004):

Automobile gas, US, unleaded, .72 to .73 (one gallon weighs 6.03 pounds)
Automobile gas, UK, .737 (one gallon weighs 6.13 pounds)
Avgas, US, .716 (one gallon weighs 5.95 pounds)
Avgas, UK, .706 (one gallon weighs 5.87 pounds)
Avgas, Australia, .672 (one gallon weighs 5.62 pounds)
Avgas, Iceland & N.Z., .755 (one gallon weighs 6.31 pounds)

These differing weights are due to differing blends and additives. For most general aviation aircraft, using 6 pounds per US gallon will work just fine. If we have 35 gallons of fuel capacity, in Australia, our fuel will weigh 196.7 pounds, while in Iceland or New Zealand, our 35 gallons will weigh 221 pounds, a difference of 25 pounds.

The IEA says motor oil varies between .85 and .9. (One gallon weighs about 7.3 pounds.)

Jet A, UK, .81 (one gallon weighs 6.74 pounds)
Jet A, US, .79 (one gallon weighs 6.57 pounds)

If you are wondering how I got these numbers, the formula is specific gravity times 3.78 (number of liters in a gallon) times 2.2 (number of pounds in a kilogram).

With Jet A, it does make a difference because the fuel capacities of jet aircraft tend to be significantly higher. While .17 pounds (2.75 ounces) per gallon doesn't seem like much, if you are putting 20,000 gallons of fuel into your airliner, it weighs 134,800 pounds in the UK and 131,400 pounds in the US, a difference of 3,400 pounds. If a "standard" airline passenger weighs 200 pounds, that's 17 more people you can carry (and collect fares for) if you buy your fuel in the US instead of in the UK. (This "found profit" assumes the price is the same - and it isn't).

Essentially, the ARC-1 and its cousin the CRP-5 will let you do your calculations correctly anywhere in the world, while the US origin E-6B is, like most US citizens, unaware that there even is a rest of the world. (Yes, I am a US citizen.)

Here's how you do it.

We're looking for the weight of 35 US gallons of fuel, and the specific gravity of the fuel is .72. (I find this interesting. In all the years I have been buying gasoline, I have never seen the specific gravity marked on the pump, anywhere. All that's there is the octane and the price.)

Find the US Gal legend on the outside scale and rotate the inner wheel so "35" on the center scale is directly under it. You'll notice the reference line on the US Gal legend is on the left side of the red block, and that's what you put the "35" under. You can use the red alignment line on the rotating index bar to get it spot on.

Now, without moving the wheel, move the rotating index bar so the top of the red line is over "72" on the specific gravity scale for lbs. (Note there are two specific gravity scales. If you hold the flight computer with "ARC-1 flight Computer" at the top, the specific gravity scale on the right is the one you'll use if you want your answer in pounds, and the scale on the left is the one to use if you want your answer in kilograms.)

With the red line over "72" on the specific gravity in pounds scale, look down at the center scale, and you'll see the red line is just slightly to the left of (lower than) 21, which means 35 US gallons of gas, with a specific gravity of .72, weighs just about 210 pounds. (Quick check, 35 times 6 = 210.)

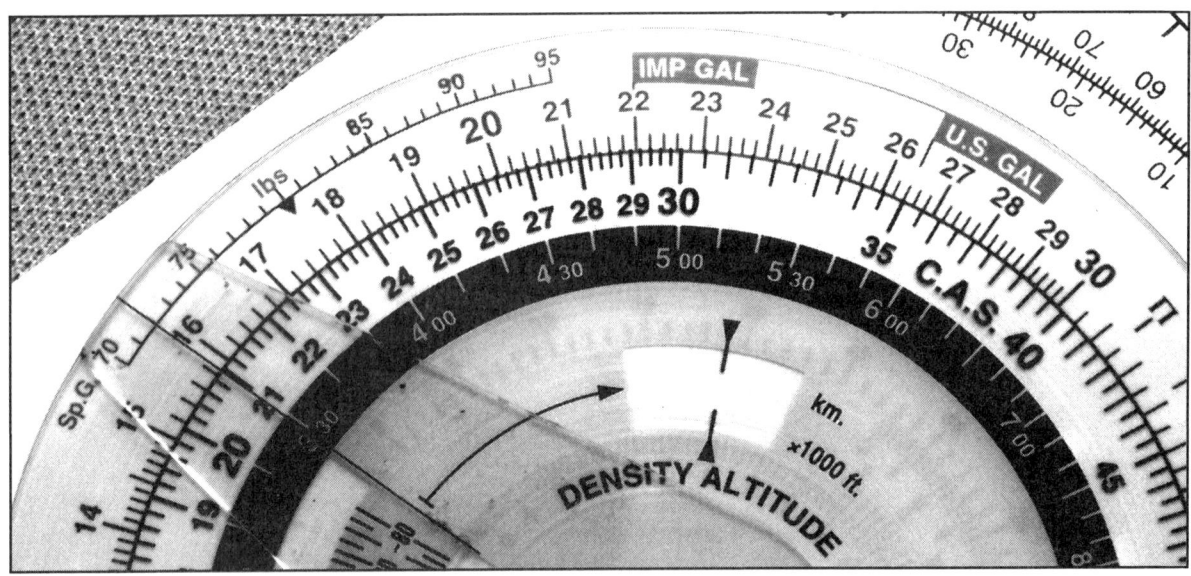

35 on center scale under US Gallons, index bar on .72 on the specific gravity scale (lbs), 21, which is really 210, on center scale under index bar. The weight of 35 US gallons of fuel is 210 pounds.

Sounds like a lot of trouble, but if we wanted the weight in kilograms, we'd move the red line over to "72" on the left (kg) scale, and discover that our 35 US gallons of gas weighs 95.5 kg. (Quick check, 95.5 times 2.2 = 210, so we are right on the money). We note that there is no 72 on the kgs scale, just 70 and 75, so we have to estimate.

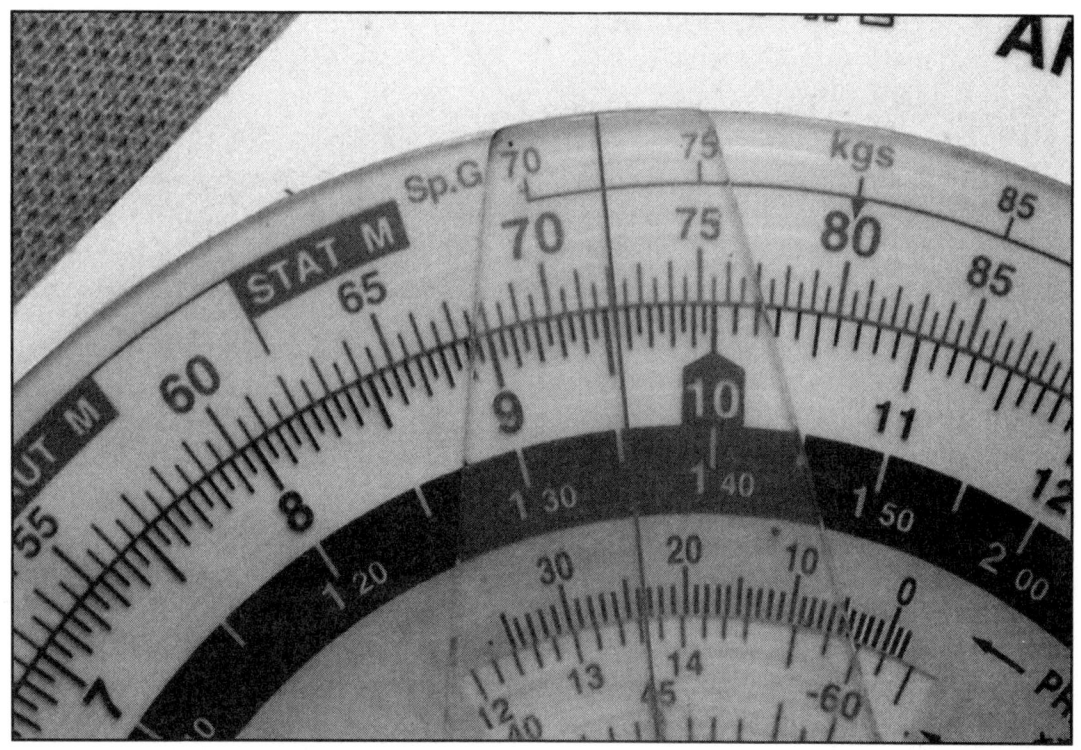

35 on the center scale is still under US Gallons, but we have moved the index bar to .72 on the specific gravity scale for kg. The answer is 95.5 kg, which is right at 210 pounds.

I suppose that to be perfectly correct, I should use the word "petrol" in the above paragraphs instead of the word "gas", but since we are talking about US gallons, "gas" will do.

Remember that we can use "72" for the specific gravity of fuel both in the US and the UK, but now let's try it for Australia (sg=.672) and Iceland (sg=.755)

Australia first: 35 on center scale under US gal line on outer scale, red line over "67" on sg scale for lbs (Hey, it doesn't go there! You'll have to estimate.), answer on center scale is about 194 to 196 pounds.

Iceland: 35 on center scale under US gal line on outer scale, red line over 755 on sg scale for lbs, answer about 220 lbs. Easy.

Function 4: Time, Speed, Distance

Basic Time, Speed and Distance calculations

It is always easier to learn something going from what you know toward what you don't know, and time, speed and distance calculations are no exception.

We do time, speed and distance calculations every day. We might say the airport is "an hour away" based on an average speed of 60 miles an hour, and the airport is 60 miles away. Similarly, we say, "It is 30 miles, it will take us about an hour to get there" which means we expect our average speed to be about 30 miles an hour.

The E-6B easily solves these problems when the numbers aren't even, or are not familiar.

Lets do some easy ones first, and we will put the numbers into the E-6B (or ARC-1 or CRP-1) so you can see what the "picture" looks like. We are going 70 miles an hour, we have 210 miles to go, it will take three hours, which is the same as 180 minutes. Agreed?

If we had to work this out in our heads, we would have no trouble saying things like "at 70 mph it will take three hours to go 210 miles" or "to go 210 miles in three hours we have to average 70 mph" and so on. Notice that if you have any two of the time, the speed, or the distance, you can always find the third.

So pick up the wheel, and point the rate index (black arrow on E-6B, white 60/1 triangle on ARC-1 and CRP-1) to "70" on the outside scale. The "rate index" is the "how fast?" marker. This rate index should always point to the speed. (Note that I have also seen a CRP-1 with a red triangle for a rate index.)

Now find 210 on the outside scale. Read inward on the wheel to the minutes scale and find 180, and then read further inward to the hours scale and find 3. We had the speed and the distance, and we just found the time, expressed as minutes and as hours.

Let's work this backwards. We have to go 210 miles, and we have to do it in three hours. Find the 210 (distance) on the outside scale, and place the time (three hours) directly under it. Guess what? The rate index now points to the speed: 70 miles an hour! In this case we had the time and the distance, and we found the speed.

Finally, if we go 70 mph for three hours, what's the distance? Rate index to 70 (speed), find three hours on the hours scale, read out to the distance scale. Answer, 210 miles.

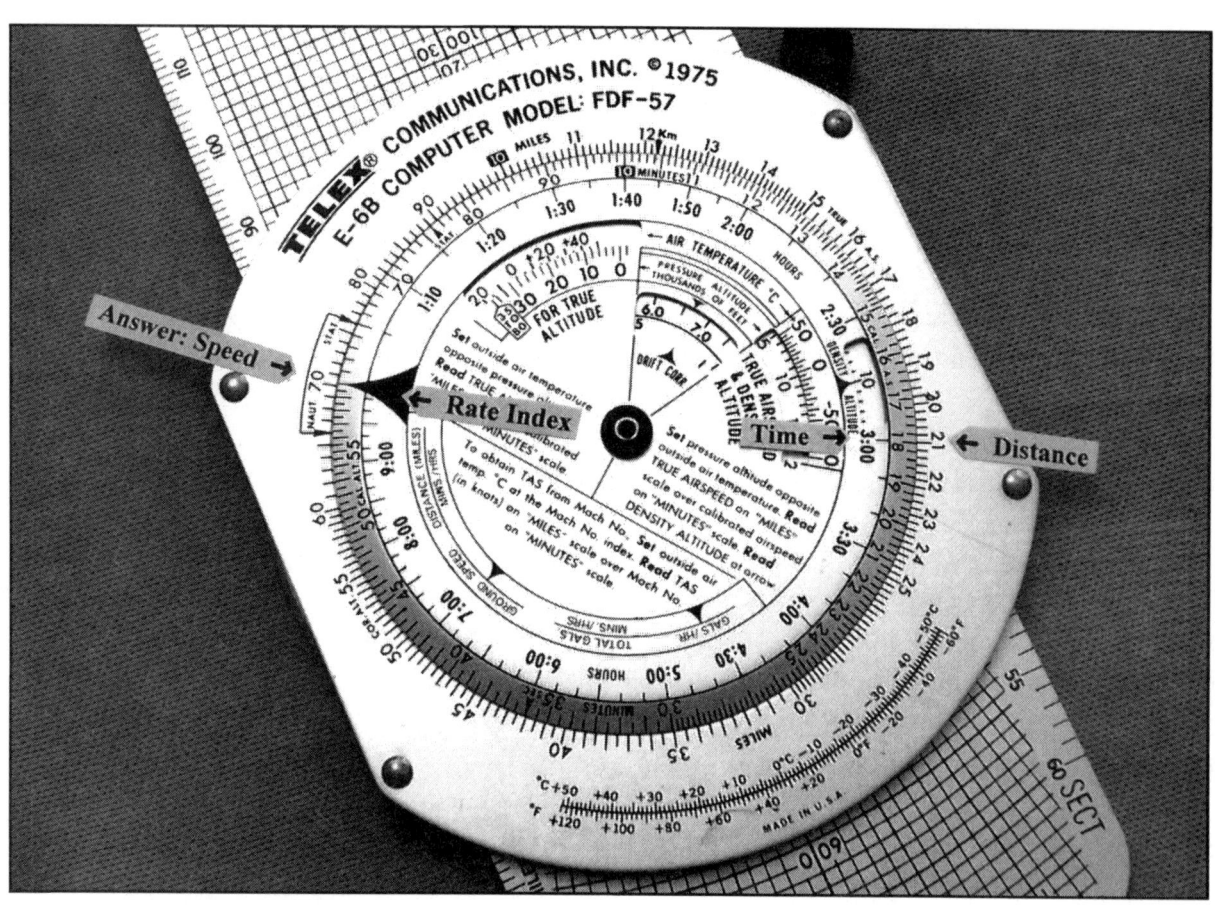

We set the time, 3 hours, under the distance, 210 miles, and read the answer above the rate index; 70 miles an hour.

Here's one with numbers that don't come out so easily. We're going 85 knots indicated air speed, we have 116 nautical miles to go. How long will this take (no wind)?

Rate index points to 85, find 116 on outside scale, read 82 minutes on the minutes scale, or keep reading down to the hours scale and read one hour 22 minutes. (If you got an hour and 54 minutes, you are looking at 160 for your distance instead of 116. Common error, so be careful!)

Next question (on next page): We've gone 300 miles in an hour and ten minutes, so how fast are we going? We can't point the rate index to the speed because we don't know the speed. Remember that on the other problems, when the rate index pointed to the speed, the time and the distance lined up, so lets try this one backwards. If we line up the time and the distance, we should be able to find the speed.

Start with 30 on the outside ring, remembering that 30 is really 300, and line up 70 on the minutes scale. 70 is of course an hour and ten minutes expressed as minutes. Where does the rate index point? Directly at 257 miles an hour, and that's the answer.

(Illustration on facing page.)

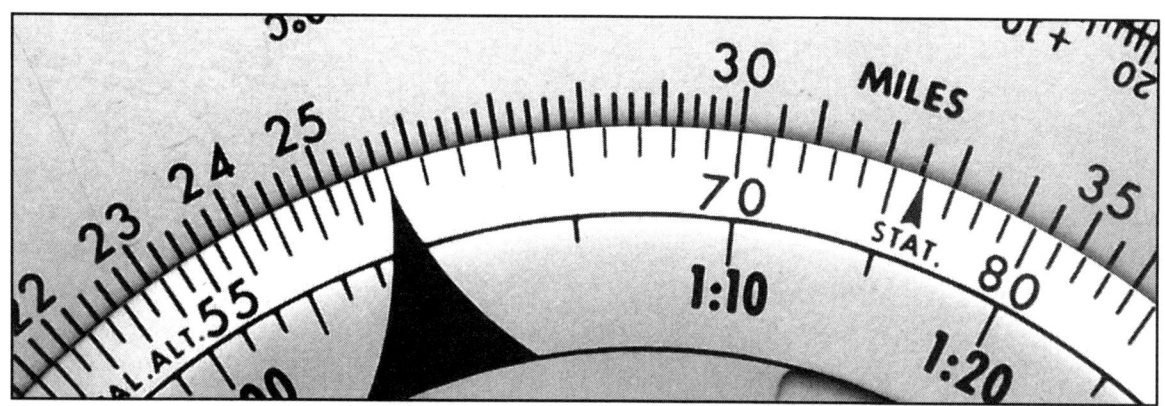

Finally, how about going a little faster? Our airplane goes 450 KIAS, and we have 732 nautical miles to go. How long will this take? (Assume no wind, which is nonsense, because there is always wind, and most of the time it is a headwind. Rats.)

Rate index on 45 (which we know is actually 450), find 73.2 on the outside scale, read down to 98 minutes, which is an hour and 38 minutes. Nice ride!

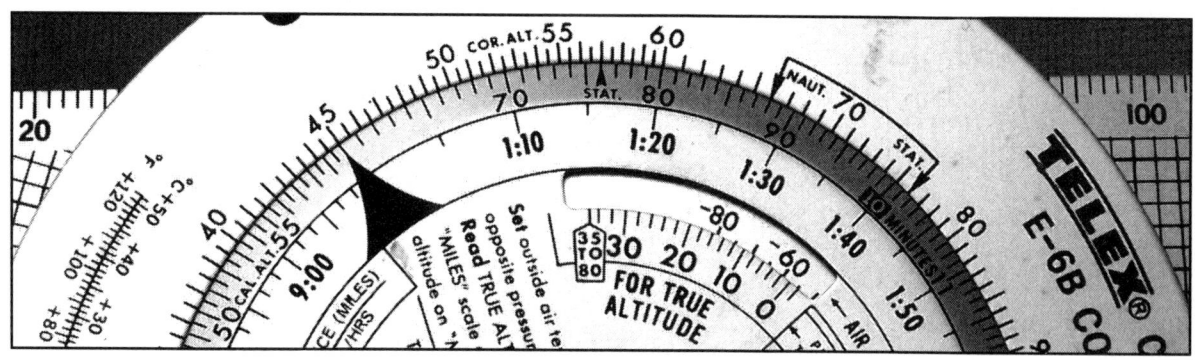

Function 5: Fuel Use

Fuel Consumption Problems

Fuel consumption problems are done exactly the same way as time, speed and distance problems. You will recall we used the outside scale for speed and distance, and the two inner scales for time. When we do fuel consumption problems, the outside scale is now gallons per hour and total consumed, and the two inside scales are still time, same as they were before. The rate index is now used for fuel use, and it answers the question "how many gallons per hour?" (rate of use) instead of "how fast? (rate of speed).

Starting with what we know, our airplane burns seven gallons per hour, so in three hours we will use 21 gallons of fuel. Alternatively, 21 gallons of fuel will last three hours at a rate of seven gallons an hour. Finally, if we used 21 gallons in three hours, the rate was seven GPH. (Do these numbers sound familiar?)

Second situation: Our airplane burns 12 GPH and carries 65 usable gallons of fuel, how long before the noise stops? Index on 12, find 65 on outside scale, answer ~~330~~ 325 minutes, which is five hours 30 minutes.

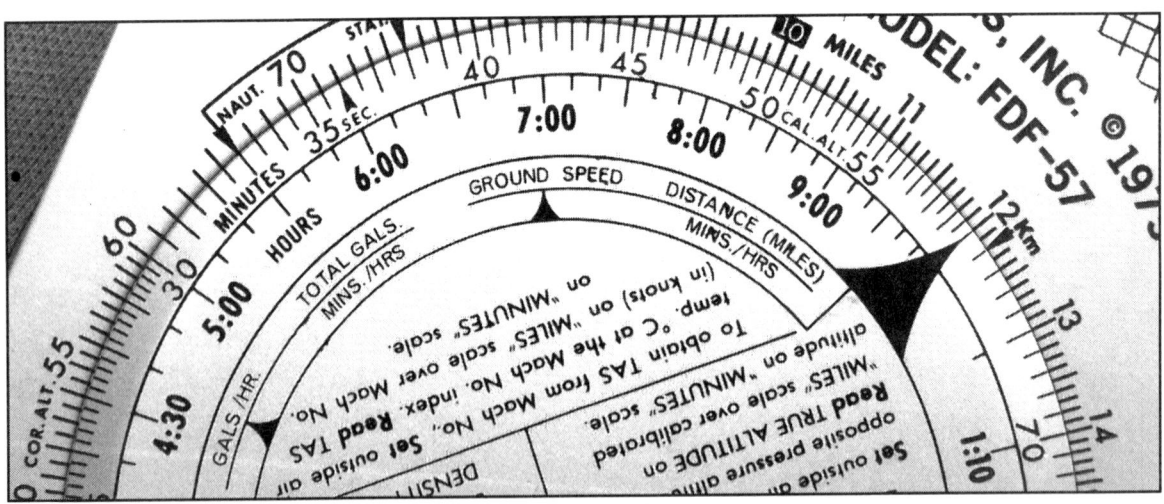

Rate index set to 12 (g.p.h.), find 5 h ~~30~~ 25 m under 65 (gallons) on the outside scale.

We do not, however, wish to fly until the noise stops. We want to have reserves, which will give us time (fuel is time) to find more fuel before we have a glider. In the USA, daytime VFR reserves are 30 minutes, and nighttime VFR reserves are 45 minutes. At 12 gallons per hour, we need to "reserve" six gallons during the day, and nine gallons at night. This makes our usable fuel 59 gallons when the sun is up and 56 when it is not.

What does that do to our flight time? At 12 GPH (rate index on 12) find 59 on the outside scale, and read inward to find 294 minutes, which is four hours (240 minutes) and 54 minutes. That's cutting things a bit close, and I would prefer to start looking for more fuel at about four hours 30 minutes, which is a long time nonstop in a small airplane.

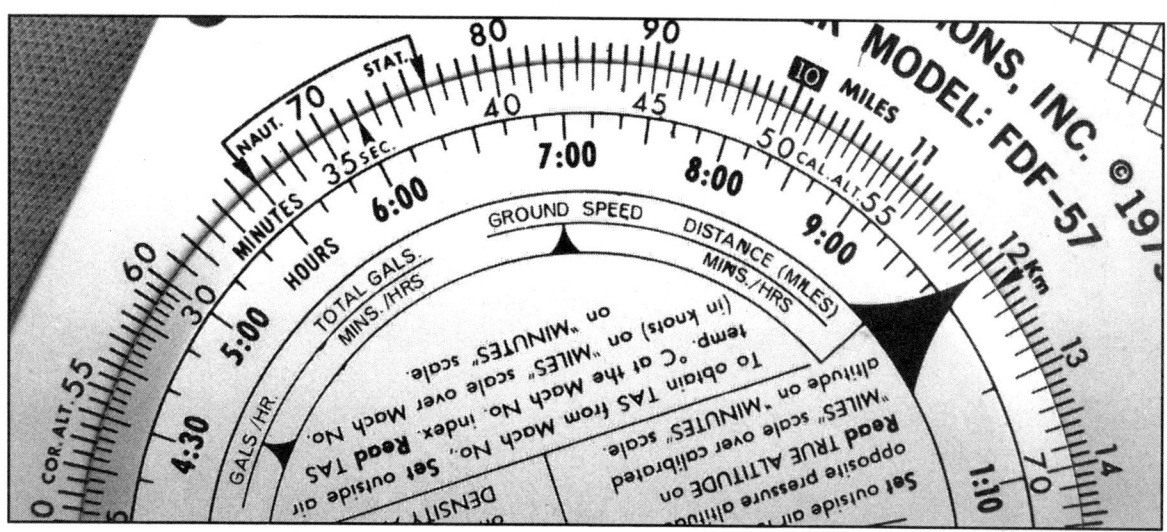

Rate still at 12 (g.p.h.), but find 4 h 54 m under 59 (gallons usable) on outside scale.

At night, we are "on reserve" at four hours 40 minutes, but that's really pushing your luck, so I'd start looking for fuel at about four hours total time. It seems airports and fuel supplies (like bathrooms) are inversely proportional to how desperately you need them.

Doing it this way is putting the cart before the horse anyway. In this airplane, we would plan our flights so that during the day, each leg might be just a bit over four hours, and at night, perhaps slightly less than four hours.

The problem is wind. A headwind reduces our still-air range by the speed of the wind times the number of hours we are in it. Our airplane goes 150 miles an hour, so if there were no wind, in four hours we'd go 600 miles. If we have a 30 mile per hour headwind (not unusual), in four hours we'd cover only 480 miles (600 minus four times 30), and we would have burned the same 48 gallons of fuel to do it. Remember, fuel is always *time*, and it is *never range*.

This is the reason we do wind triangle problems. They tell us the effective headwinds (or if we are lucky, tailwinds), and we can adjust our fuel stop intervals accordingly so we never run low or out of fuel. Always remember that one of the three most useless things in aviation is fuel still in the truck, with the other two being the altitude above you and the runway behind you.

We should do a few more fuel use problems because we want to get good at this.

The next airplane burns 32 gallons an hour, and the fuel totalizer tells us we have used 27.5 gallons. How long have we been flying? Rate index on 32, read inward from 27.5, answer is about 51.5 minutes. (No one brought a wristwatch? The airplane is required to have a clock, too, and it is supposed to work. Now you know why.)

Rate index on 32 (ignore the word "miles"), read 51.5 m under 27.5 (gallons) on outside scale.

Try these yourself:

8 GPH, 2.5 hours	(answer: 20 gallons required)
12.5 GPH, 27 minutes	(answer: 5.65 gallons required)
55 GPH, 2 hours 20 minutes	(answer: 128 gallons required)

In general, most trainers burn five to ten gallons an hour, and go between 80 and 120 miles an hour. The world's most popular trainer, the venerable Cessna 150, burns five and a half to six gallons an hour. Cherokees and 172s are somewhat thirstier, but not hugely so. Unfortunately, the E-6B will not tell you how to pay for the fuel. You have to work this out on your own.

Function 6: Wind Triangles

Wind triangles demystified

Understand that if you ask a hundred licensed pilots how to do a wind triangle, you'll get 362 different and conflicting answers. A few of them may even be correct.

Figuring wind triangles has fallen into disuse for several reasons. If you fly following roads, and many of us do, then you won't need wind triangles at all. The road will take you where you want to go, and from time to time you will notice that the airplane isn't lined up with the road even though it is traveling along it. This is the effect of the wind. To compensate, we crab the airplane into the wind so our path over the ground is what we want, even if the nose isn't pointed exactly towards where we are going.

If you are flying real IFR (as opposed to the above example, which is known as "I Follow Roads"), your various navigation instruments will keep your track correct. Keeping the VOR needle centered means you are definitely on the selected radial, and if the nose of the airplane isn't pointed directly at or directly away from the VOR station, that doesn't matter. You are traveling directly along the radial anyway.

We need wind triangles in areas that have few or no landmarks (like oceans), or that are out of range of navigational equipment (with GPS, this isn't a problem), or if we should have an electrical failure in flight. This failure can be as simple as someone pushed the wrong button on the audio panel, or a blown fuse or popped breaker. The result is the VOR and any other navigational equipment powered by the aircraft's electrical system are now inop, and if there are no landmarks, you are absolutely on your own and working with the compass. Somehow I do not find myself enthused with the idea of finding one small island in the middle of the shark-filled sea by reference to only a compass. (This makes quite a strong case for a hand-held battery powered GPS . . . $100 at the nearest sporting goods or boating supply store. Get some spare batteries, too.)

In this case, the wind triangle we did as part of our flight plan BEFORE we got off the ground is what will save our hides. When everything is working, take note of the compass heading. That's the direction the nose of the airplane is pointed to, and is not necessarily the track over the ground. If the wind triangle was done correctly (and the winds aloft don't change, and we don't change our cruise speed), even though the navigation equipment has made a square purple smoke ring and died, by holding the compass heading we previously calculated, we will (very likely) arrive close enough to our destination to be able to find the airport.

If we didn't do the wind triangle, we have nothing to fall back on and could easily be in a heap of trouble.

Here is how we can visualize a wind triangle. We are flying directly to the north at 100 miles an hour, and the wind is blowing directly from the east at 30 miles an hour. If we fly with the nose of the airplane pointed directly to the north, at the end of 100 miles, we will be 30 miles west of where we wanted to be.

However, if we point the nose to the north-east (more or less), we will counter the effect of the wind, and our track over the ground will be directly north, which is what we wanted in the first place. The airplane is pointed somewhat to the northeast, but is traveling to the north. There is also an effect on our ground speed. This doesn't seem to make sense because the wind is directly abeam, not a headwind or a tailwind, but it does affect the ground speed.

Using the wind side of the E-6B, we set it up as follows:

1) Place the wind direction (090) under the index.

Wind direction of 090 (E) under true index.

2) Move the slider card so 100 is under the center hole (this makes your math easier).

(Illustration next page)

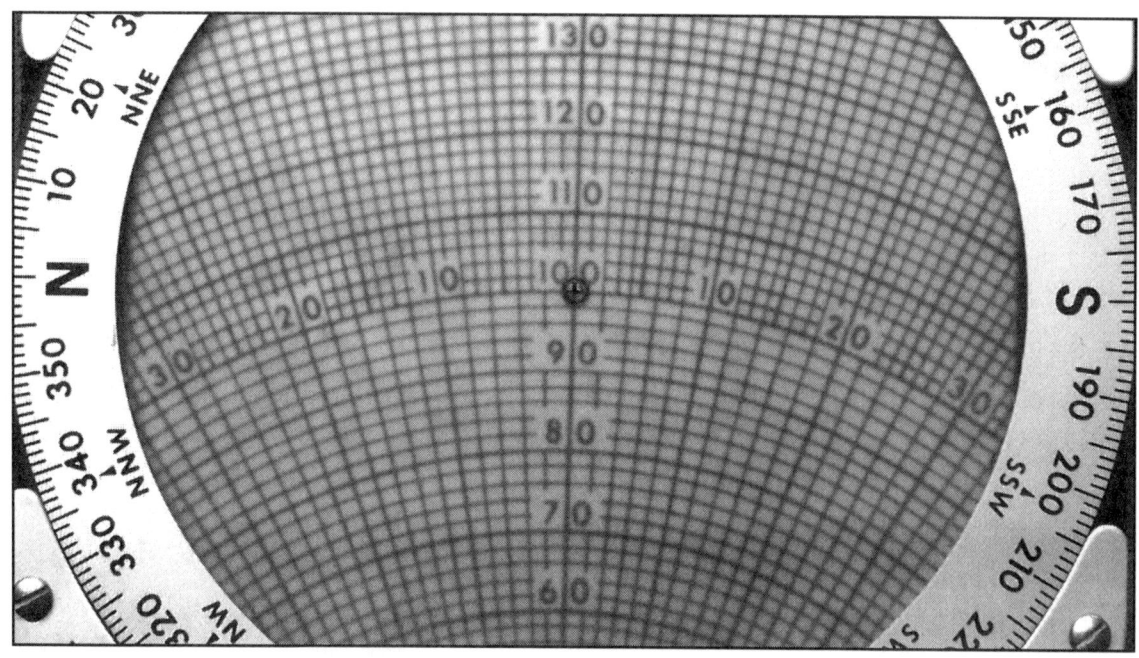

Set slider card so 100 is under the center hole.

3) Make a pencil dot at 130 (We will use the 100 as zero, plus the 30 miles an hour wind speed). Note - use a *PENCIL* to make the dot. If you use a pen, the ink will not come off, and the wind speed will be 30 knots for the rest of your flying career.)

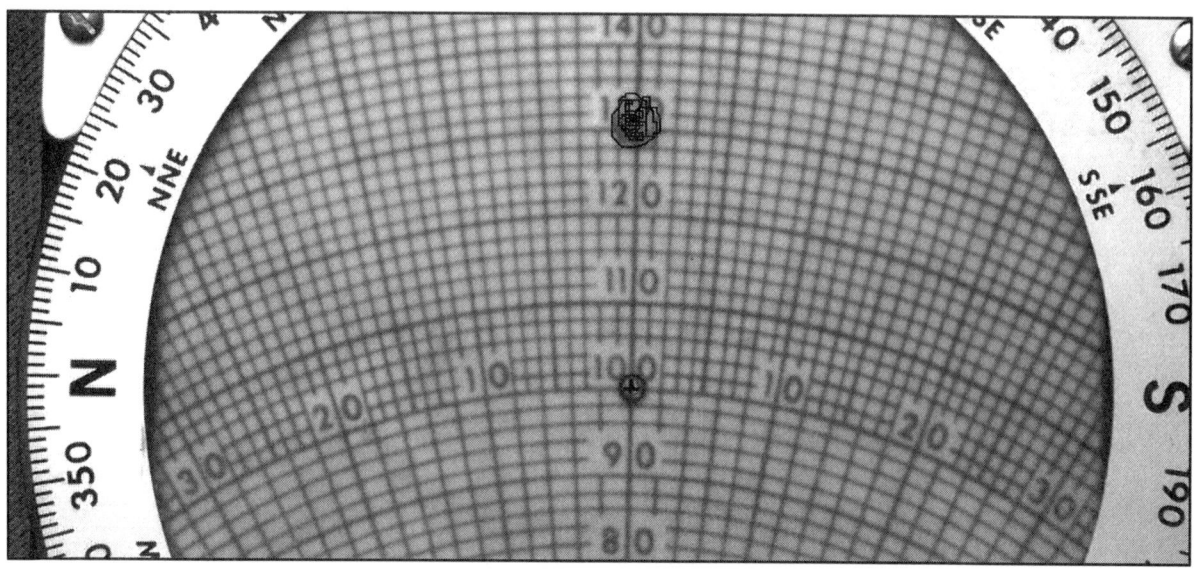

Large, ugly pencil dot at 130 (100 + 30).

4) Now place the true course under the index (rotate so 360 is under the index). Note your pencil dot has moved to the right and down.

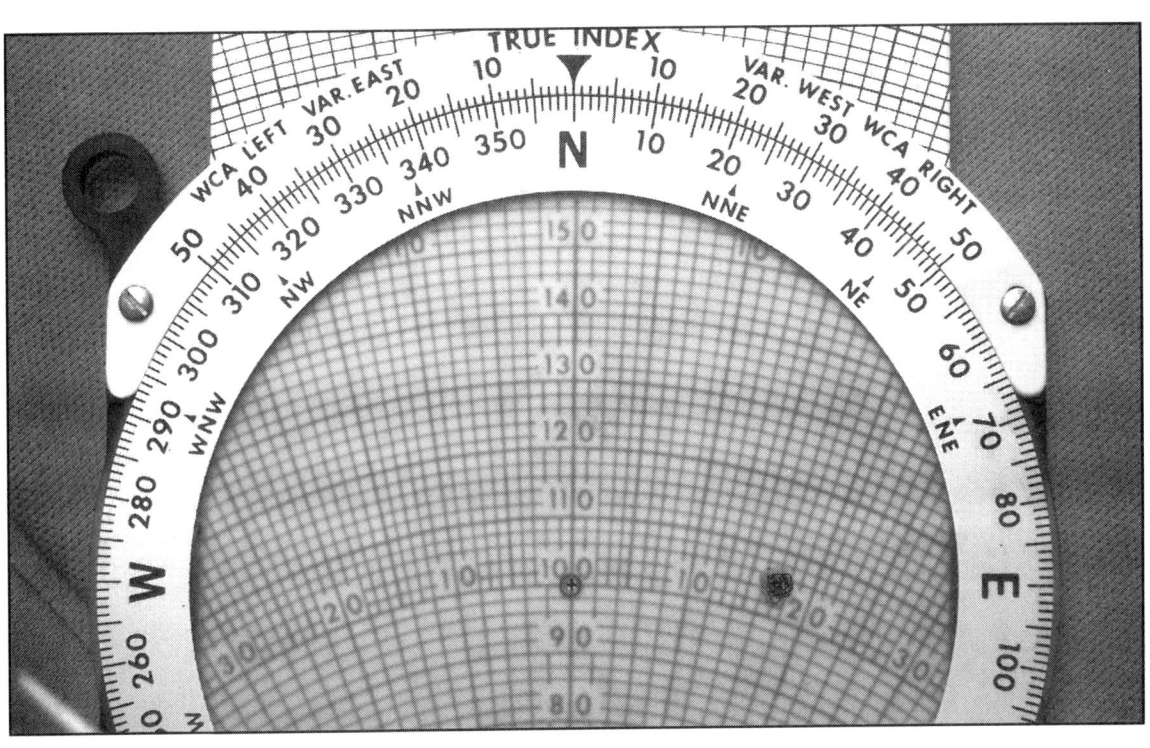

Placing 360 under true index moves the dot to the right and down.

5) Move the slider card so the 100 miles an hour air speed arc is under the pencil dot.

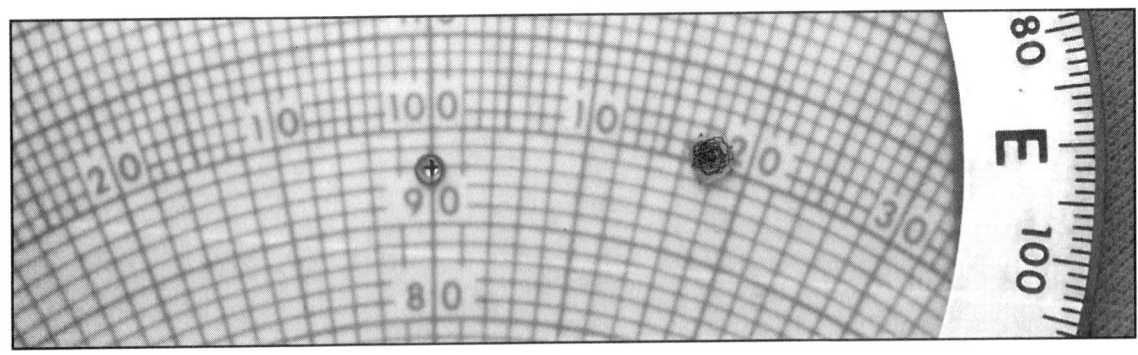

We've moved the slider card so the 100 arc is under our pencil dot.

6) Read answers: New ground speed is shown at the center, it is 95 miles an hour. The correction for the wind drift is under the dot, it is 18 degrees to the right. (Note that the dot was too large and the ground speed shows 96 instead of 95. For best results, be neater with your dot than I was.)

Therefore, if the wind is 090 at 30, our course is 360, and our airspeed is 100 miles an hour, if we turn into the wind 18 degrees (fly an indicated 018), then our track over the ground will be directly north. We also see that our ground speed has dropped to 95 miles an hour, and that means the 100 miles to the island will take one hour and three minutes.

Be careful here. If anything changes, your answers will too. In addition, this quick exercise does not mention variation and deviation, both of which affect the compass reading. It also uses the wind speed in miles an hour, and the weather people deliver it in knots. "Miles an hour" was used because everyone is familiar with that. Your actual calculations will probably be in knots since nowadays the ASI is probably in knots, and the wind is in knots. You can do this in miles an hour if you want to, but you have to convert the wind speed to miles an hour first.

Suppose we speed up to 140 miles an hour.

Steps 1 through 4 remain the same, but at step 5, we move the slider card so the IAS of 140 (instead of 100) is under the pencil dot.

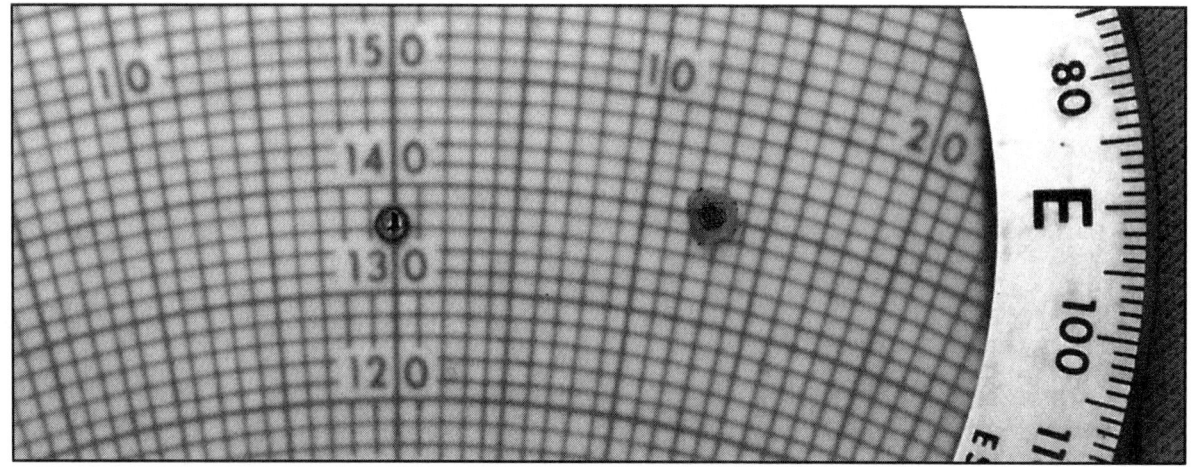

Slider card moved so our new indicated air speed of 140 is under the pencil dot.

Step 6: Read answers: New ground speed is shown at the center, it is 137 miles an hour. Correction for wind drift is under the dot, but is now only 12 to 13 degrees to the right instead of 18 degrees. (30 miles an hour wind speed is a smaller proportion of 140 miles an hour air speed than of 100 miles an hour, so less correction is needed.) Time to the island is now 43 minutes.

Notice the correction for wind drift. It is now five degrees less. This means that if you change your speed, you *must* re-figure the wind triangle, or you will not arrive where you want to.

Here's an example of how this can ambush you. We are flying directly north to a small island 120 miles offshore, well within the range of even the most modest of training aircraft. We figure our wind triangles correctly, and calculate a correction of 18 degrees based on a cruise speed of 100 miles an hour. A few minutes after we take off, all the nav equipment fails (alternator died), and for some reason (bad case of get-there-itis?) we cannot return to our point of origin.

As long as we maintain our 100 miles an hour air speed and our 18 degree correction factor (steer 018 on the compass to go 360), we are fine, and we arrive in just under an hour and a quarter.

However, we get spooked by the electrical failure and decide to get there quicker by speeding up to 140 miles an hour. If we did the wind triangle for 140 miles an hour, we would find the correction factor to be 12.5 degrees instead of 18 degrees, but we didn't.

The 120 mile trip now takes 52 minutes, but the island is nowhere to be seen! What happened? According to the venerable one in 60 rule, one degree of error gives us one mile of error after 60 miles enroute. Here we have five degrees of error, which would give us five miles of error after 60 miles, and ten miles of error after the 120 miles to the island. If the visibility is poor today, we may not be able to see ten miles, and guess what? We can't find the island! Gulp.

If we realize what has happened, we will realize that the island should be to our left. 18 degrees was too much wind correction for this new airspeed, and we are now too far to the east (to the right of where we wanted to be) of the island, so we would turn left to a heading of 270 and hold our breath until we see the island . . . we hope. As you see, it would be very easy to get rattled in this situation, and turn the wrong way, or turn too soon or too late or too little or too much, or all of the above.

If we are very, very lucky, and the weather is warm and somewhat humid, we may be able to find the island by looking for the cumulus clouds that often develop above islands in the tropics. This is because the sun heats the ground more than it heats the water, and there will be rising air over the island, which may make cumulus clouds over the island. Personally, I'd prefer much more reliable methods of navigation in this situation.

This is actually an example of extremely deficient ADM ("Aeronautic Decision Making"), which is an example of FAA-speak meaning "do you really think this is such a good idea?" Anyone who would voluntarily and knowingly embark on an over-water flight to a distant, tiny island without having working navigation equipment AND a carefully calculated flight plan is a candidate for a Darwin award, not a pilot's license.

The wind triangle is a backup plan for this situation. The real world is an imperfect place, screws do come loose, fuses blow, and pilots sometimes do start the engine (or engines) before their brain is engaged. Having a plan B is always a good idea. Having a plan B and a handheld GPS (with fresh batteries!) is even a better idea.

Exercises:

1) Wind 060@20, course 330, 85 KIAS, distance 130 nm, 6 gph.

Find ground speed, time, fuel required, wind correction angle and correct heading.

(Answers: no fair peeking! GS 83 knots, time 94 minutes, fuel required 9.4 gallons, WCA 14° right (+14), correct heading ~~334~~°.)

344°

2) Wind 240@30, course 200, 120 KIAS, distance 210 nm, 9.2 gph.

Find ground speed, time, fuel required, wind correction angle and correct heading.

(Answers: GS 95 knots, time 2 h 13 m, fuel required is 20.6 gallons, WCA 9° right (+9), correct heading 209°.)

3) Now we'll go home. Only the heading changes, it is now 020°.

Find ground speed, time, fuel required, wind correction angle and correct heading.

(Answers: GS 141 knots - whee! - time is 1 h 30 m, fuel required 13.8 gallons, WCA 9° left (-9), correct heading 011°.)

Function 7: Density Altitude

Density Altitude, and the Importance Thereof

The effects of Density Altitude and its importance are frequently not well understood. The very definition of Density Altitude incorporates another somewhat arcane term, and since people have a tendency to let someone else demonstrate their ignorance first, many times no one in the class (and that sometimes includes the instructor) may really understand Density Altitude or why it is important.

Here's the definition: "Density Altitude is Pressure Altitude adjusted for non-standard temperature." OK, that's nice, now what does that actually mean?

We need to dissect this definition, and we need to understand both the concept as well as the practical application. After all, we don't want to wrinkle up all that shiny aluminum, especially if we are inside of it at the time.

Lets sneak up on this from behind, and start with "standard temperature". A standard day is defined (ad nauseum) as 29.92 inches of Mercury at 59 degrees F, or 1,013.25 millibars at 15 degrees C, these being the average barometric pressure and temperature in the temperate latitudes, 20 to 40 degrees north and south of the equator.

These values are only at sea level, which is sometimes not stressed, and it should be. If we are not at sea level, the numbers are going to be different. Air pressure, or the barometric pressure, decreases about one inch of Mercury (or 37 millibars) per 1,000 feet, and as you know, the temperature decreases by 2 degrees C per thousand feet.

A "standard day" at 10,000 feet turns out to be 19.92 inches of Mercury at 23 degrees F (or about 700 mb - actually 678 mb - at about minus 5 degrees C). This is "pressure altitude", which is defined as the barometric pressure (and temperature) we expect to find at altitude X on a standard day. Therefore, if the temperature and barometric pressure are standard, the pressure altitude and the actual altitude will be the same.

Alas, any given day is almost never standard. Hot air is less dense ("thinner") than cold air, and cold air is denser than hot air. If the temperature is lower than standard for the particular altitude we are talking about, the air will be denser than standard for that particular altitude. If the temperature is higher than standard for the altitude we are talking about, the air will be less dense ("thinner") than standard for that altitude.

Airplanes like air. Airplane engines like air even more. Your mighty BugSmasher 200B, which develops its full rated horsepower at sea level, will produce perhaps 70 percent of it at 10,000 feet MSL, and perhaps less. Try a takeoff some time with the throttle only three quarters open - or better yet, don't try it, and just take my word for it that your airplane's performance will be anemic, to say the least.

At sea level on a standard day, your airplane will climb at 750 feet per minute. At 10,000 feet, your climb rate might be down to just 150 or 200 feet a minute, and that assumes the day is standard - which is a BIG assumption. There's nothing wrong with the airplane, it is just that the engine has less air to work with, so it makes less horsepower.

Since an airplane climbs if it has more horsepower than it needs to maintain level flight, if it is using all of the available horsepower just to maintain this level flight, there isn't any left over to climb, hence, you won't. Incidentally, this is known as the absolute ceiling for the airplane - you are not going any higher, period.

Anyway, as the temperature rises, the air becomes less dense, so even though we are still physically at 10,000 feet MSL, the density altitude, or the altitude the airplane thinks it is at, may be significantly higher.

If we learn to fly in Florida, where in fact 20% of the flight training in the world is done (FAA figures), we seldom go to 10,000 feet MSL. There's little need to, even though the view is pretty spectacular. Climb performance at 10,000 feet MSL isn't important to us since Florida doesn't have any mountains we need to fly over. As a result, the entire concept of density altitude tends to get glossed over in ground school. This is a big mistake, because eventually our hero pilot is going to fly someplace that isn't at sea level and isn't flat, and will suddenly discover he has a real problem, and right now!

For example, the highest civil airfield in the USA (in fact, in North America) is Leadville, Colorado, where the airport elevation is a stunning 9,927 feet MSL - you're at 10,000 feet, and you're still on the ground. The highest civil airfield in the USA with scheduled service is Telluride, Colorado, at 9,078 feet MSL. Standard temperatures at these airports are about 23 degrees F and 25 degrees F, respectively.

Both Leadville and Telluride airports were built by chopping the top off the lowest mountain they could find. The runways are short, and both airports have other, higher mountains surrounding them. This means that once you do get off the ground, you have to climb for adequate terrain clearance, and at 150 feet per minute (and decreasing as you ascend), it may take a while. Remember you only have 70% of your sea level horsepower available up here at 10,000 feet MSL, and that is if the day is standard.

Now lets try a takeoff from Leadville on a hot summer day. The OAT (outside air temperature) today isn't 23 degrees F, it is 103 degrees F. The air is going to be a lot less dense at this high temperature, so our airplane's performance, which isn't impressive at 10,000 feet MSL at 23 degrees F, is going to be a lot worse.

How much worse? Using our E-6B, we discover that the density altitude, or the effective altitude (or the altitude the airplane thinks it is at) at 10,000 feet MSL (actual altitude) on a 103 degree F day (temperature much hotter than standard, hence the air is much less dense than standard) is equivalent to a whopping 14,500 feet MSL. Your rate of climb may very well be preceded by a "minus" sign - and that isn't good.

So lets take the explanations and plug them into the definition. Density Altitude (the effective altitude, or the altitude the airplane thinks it is at) is pressure altitude (the barometric pressure we expect to find at this physical altitude on a standard day) adjusted for today's non-standard temperature.

Simply stated, if it is hotter than standard, the density altitude will be higher than the physical altitude, and the airplane's performance will be poorer than what we could expect at this altitude on a standard day. Conversely, if it is colder than standard, the density altitude will be lower than the physical altitude, and the airplane will perform better than it would at this altitude if the temperature were standard.

No one complains when it is colder than standard. I have never heard anyone say that their airplane climbs too well, and frankly, I don't ever expect to hear it, either.

When it is hotter than standard, however, this reduced performance becomes downright dangerous. With reduced power output, you'll need a longer runway, sometimes a lot longer, and once off the ground (and you may not even be able to get off the ground!), you may have insufficient performance to climb over obstacles - which is a nice way of saying you'll hit the trees because you just couldn't climb over them.

Not getting off the ground at all may be as bad as getting off the ground and then finding out you can't climb out of ground effect. Once in the air, the tendency is to want to stay there, so here's what can happen. A) The takeoff is continued, the airplane will not gain altitude, and winds up in the trees off the end of the runway. B) The takeoff is continued, the airplane will not gain altitude, the trees are getting closer, so the pilot hauls back on the yoke to climb over them - and as soon as the airplane is out of ground effect, it stalls, and there is insufficient altitude for recovery. Option A stinks, and so does option B.

Think about this - if the density altitude is such that the best rate of climb your airplane can achieve is 40 FPM, at 60 KIAS, you will gain only about 40 feet of altitude while traveling a mile. If there is a six foot chain link fence at the end of the runway, which is going to be a short runway to start with, you'll need to be off the ground for at least 925 feet before you reach a whole six feet of altitude and clear the fence by an inch. Do you feel comfortable with that? I sure don't. (6,080 feet divided by 40 is 152 feet traveled horizontally for every foot of altitude gained. We need six feet and one inch, so 6 times 152 is 912 feet, add 12.6 feet more for the last inch of clearance - that is TOO close!)

There is one question that does need to be answered, and that is how the heck did you get your airplane into this high elevation airport in the first place?

For the inbound leg, you had quite a bit of time and distance to climb to sufficient altitude for terrain and obstacle clearance, and you were also burning off fuel during the flight. You probably arrived early in the morning, when the temperature was still quite cold (lower than standard), so you had everything working for you. You had time, distance, a low density altitude, and the airplane was light. It is also very easy to go down, all you have to do is close the throttle, and it works every time.

Now it is time to leave. It is mid-afternoon, so the temperature is higher, probably as hot as it is going to be today, so you have a high density altitude. You've refueled the airplane, so the airplane is heavy. You need to climb over the obstacles, and they are close to the end of the runway, so you have neither time nor distance working for you. It is harder to go up than to go down, and if your horsepower needs require opening the throttle beyond "all the way", well, you're out of luck.

So why then, are not all the high elevation airports in the world simply littered with airplanes that got in and now can't get back out again? How DO we get back out again?

We send whoever and whatever we can back by other means (mail or bus, for instance), we plan a flight to the nearest lower elevation airfield where we can refuel, we carry only enough fuel to get there (plus reserves), and we leave early in the morning, when it is really, really cold so the density altitude is lower than the physical altitude. This gives us adequate performance so we can take off, establish a positive rate of climb adequate for terrain and obstacle clearance, and fly to the lower elevation airfield where we can pick up our passenger(s), our "stuff" and then add sufficient fuel to get home.

The three "H"s in combination will get you every time - Hot, High, and Heavy. High we are stuck with since we can't lower the airfield. Hot we can deal with by waiting until it is cold, as in wait until tomorrow morning. Heavy we can deal with by carrying just enough fuel (plus reserves) to get to the lower elevation airfield where the air is dense enough to restore our accustomed performance and the attendant safety margins.

While it may be even colder at night than early in the morning, taking off at night in an airplane with marginal performance over unlit mountainous terrain does not seem to be a recipe for long life and happiness. Wait until the morning so you can see where you're going, even if it is a few degrees warmer.

A few words are in order about the performance figures shown in the POH. These numbers were arrived at a long time ago (and sometimes, it seems, in a galaxy far, far away). They are the average figures for a brand new airplane flown by a skilled test pilot, and may or may not have been "enhanced" slightly (or sometimes more than slightly) by the sales department. The airplane YOU are flying TODAY may still match them, but to be on the safe side, assume it will not. Be conservative, you'll live longer. Hint - know your airplane!!!

When we figure the density altitude on our E-6B, we have two things working against us. First, we'll need a magnifying glass, because the markings are very small and very close together, which makes them hard to read. Second, because they are so small, we tend to think that they must not be very important, because if they were important, they would be larger, right?

After all that, performing the actual calculation is pretty simple. We line up the elevation (or the altitude) with the outside air temperature in the right hand window, and then read the density altitude in the window to the left of it. Simple, really.

Using the example above, at Leadville, Colorado (9,927 feet MSL) and the temperature at 103 degrees F, we first convert 103 degrees F to C. This is found on the temperature conversion scale, and we see that 103 degrees F is equal to just under 40 degrees C.

Now we find +40 on the air temperature scale, and turn the wheel so it is above 10 on the pressure altitude scale. The answer is in the density altitude window, and it is 15,000 feet. Be careful since the markings are really small and close together - and your life may depend on it.

Let's go to Telluride (9,078 feet MSL) with an OAT of 80 degrees F. The temperature is +27C, so we line up +27 with 9, and the density altitude is "only" 12,500 feet. Tomorrow morning, when it is -15F, that gives us a density altitude of about 6,500 feet, the airplane practically leaps into the air, and we wonder what all the fuss was about.

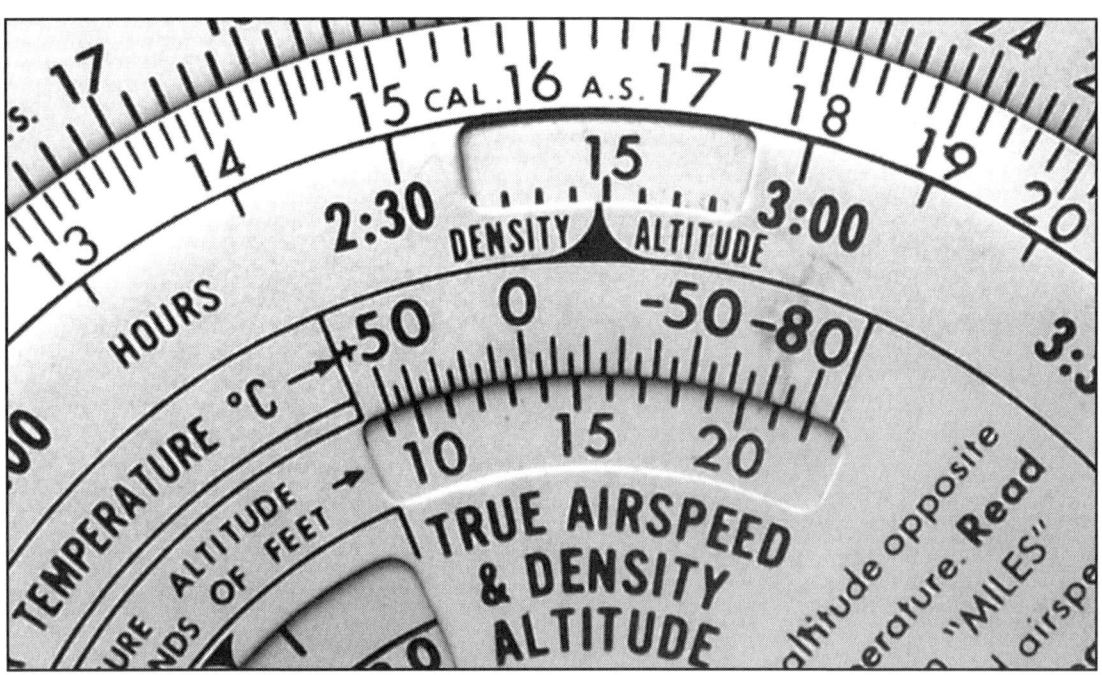

A hot day at Leadville. Put +40°C over "10" in the window, and read the density altitude in the "density altitude" window above the arrow. Just under 15,000 feet. Gulp.

Telluride: Put +27°C over "9" in the window, and read the density altitude in the "density altitude" window above the arrow. This time it is "only" 12,500 feet. Are we scared? We should be.

Function 8: True Altitude

Question: How high are we? (Remember we are talking about airplanes here . . .) Pressure altitude is 9,000 feet, OAT is -15 C. What's the real altitude?

Answer from the E-6B: Align 9,000 feet in pressure altitude window on left, against -15C air temperature window also on left. Read 9,000 feet on center scale, find 8,600 feet on outer scale, that is our true altitude.

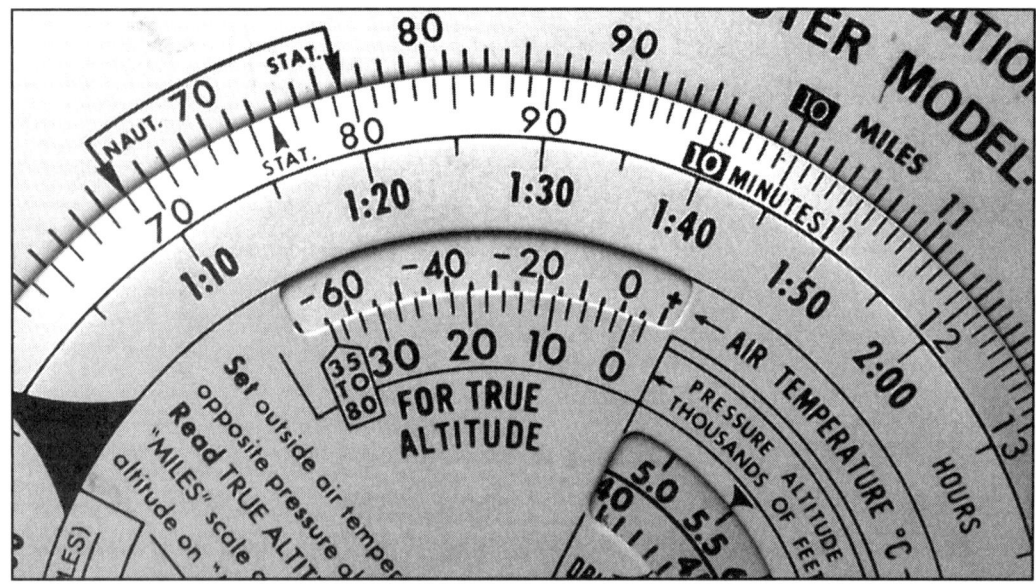

Look closely at this, it is confusing. We read from the inside outward. The pressure altitude is what the altimeter says, 9,000 feet. We move the wheel so 9,000 feet (innermost scale) is under the OAT, which is -15C (next scale out). Then we find 9,000 feet (90) on the minutes scale, and read the actual altitude on the outside scale. We are at 8,600 feet MSL (shows as 86).

Real Answer: Probably somewhere near about the indicated altitude, more or less, give or take, plus or minus or so. Remember that everyone else flying in our immediate vicinity has the same pressure altitude and temperature, and if we are ALL off the same amount and in the same direction, we won't be running into each other.

The altimeter tells us the height above MSL. It has a sealed brass capsule (the aneroid capsule) which responds to changes in barometric pressure by expanding when the air pressure decreases around it ("the air is thin, so we must be high") or contracting when the air pressure around it increases ("the air is dense, so we must be low"), and the amount of this expansion or contraction is indicated on a dial which is marked off in feet.

The instrument itself is supposed to be accurate to within 20 feet at the low end, and to within 180 feet at an indicated 20,000 feet. Unfortunately, these errors are frequently not linear, and you might have an instrument which reads a bit high at some altitudes and a bit low at others. Tolerances are allowed to increase with altitude since there's very little to run into at 20,000 feet MSL.

Since the instrument measures ambient air pressure, it requires an undisturbed area of air to take the reading. This is not as easy as it sounds since an airplane in flight disturbs the air around it, sometimes by quite a lot.

Here are two pictures of an airplane that disturbed the air around it by quite a lot. Heck, it disturbs me just to look at it. This is the Linke-Hoffman R-1 from 1917, equipped with four 230 hp Mercedes engines driving two propellers. It was so ugly that the entire rear half of the aircraft was covered in cellophane possibly in a vain attempt to make it less visible, or perhaps just less nauseating. If this isn't the ugliest airplane in the known universe, it is a darn good candidate. Mercifully, only a few were made.

Here is another airplane that disturbed the air around it by quite a lot, but for rather different reasons. Big, very, very fast (Mach 3+), very, very loud, and costing more than the equivalent weight in gold, this is the XB-70 Valkyrie of 1964. It is the definitive example of what happens when talented aerospace engineers are turned loose with a bottomless government checkbook and explicit instructions to "build the best". Amazing what 45 years of progress will do. Mercifully (for the taxpayers), only a few (two) were made.

The attitude of the airplane also makes a difference. Airplanes with a static port (the source for ambient air pressure) on only one side will show different instrument readings if slipped to the right or to the left.

Since the ambient air pressure changes (the barometer changes), we need to compensate for that as well. This one is easy. We set the local barometric pressure into the window before startup, and make sure the indicated altitude matches the field altitude. Alternatively, we can set the field elevation and make sure the barometric pressure window matches the altimeter setting from ATIS or the tower. Since the correct name for this instrument is a "Kollsman sensitive altimeter", the barometric pressure window is often referred to as the "Kollsman window".

Individual instruments sometimes have wear or other mechanical errors. There can be misalignment, friction or free play in the gears that raise and lower the aneroid capsule, and leaks in the static lines may also affect the readings.

Believe it or not, local terrain can affect your altimeter readings as well. The wind blowing around or over a single large mountain peak or ridge will tend to increase in speed, and decrease in pressure (Bernoulli effect!), so the local barometric pressure will be lower than the surrounding area's barometric pressure. This means your altimeter will start to read higher ("the air is thin, so we must be high") at the precise time that we need it to be accurate - there's a mountain down there, and we really, really do want adequate terrain clearance! In combination with the local drop in barometric pressure and very warm weather, your altimeter may be reading as much as 3,000 feet too high, and this is one place where you want to be very sure of your altitude.

Another similar problem arises in downdrafts and turbulence. If you are flying downwind of a mountain ridge (lower local barometric pressure courtesy of the wind, the mountain ridge and Bernoulli), and you enter a downdraft, your altimeter and VSI may actually initially indicate a climb even though the ground is getting closer and closer.

Function 9: True Air Speed, compressibility, Mach number, other fables

Question: How fast are we going? OAT is -15 C, IAS is 125 knots, pressure altitude is 8,000 feet.

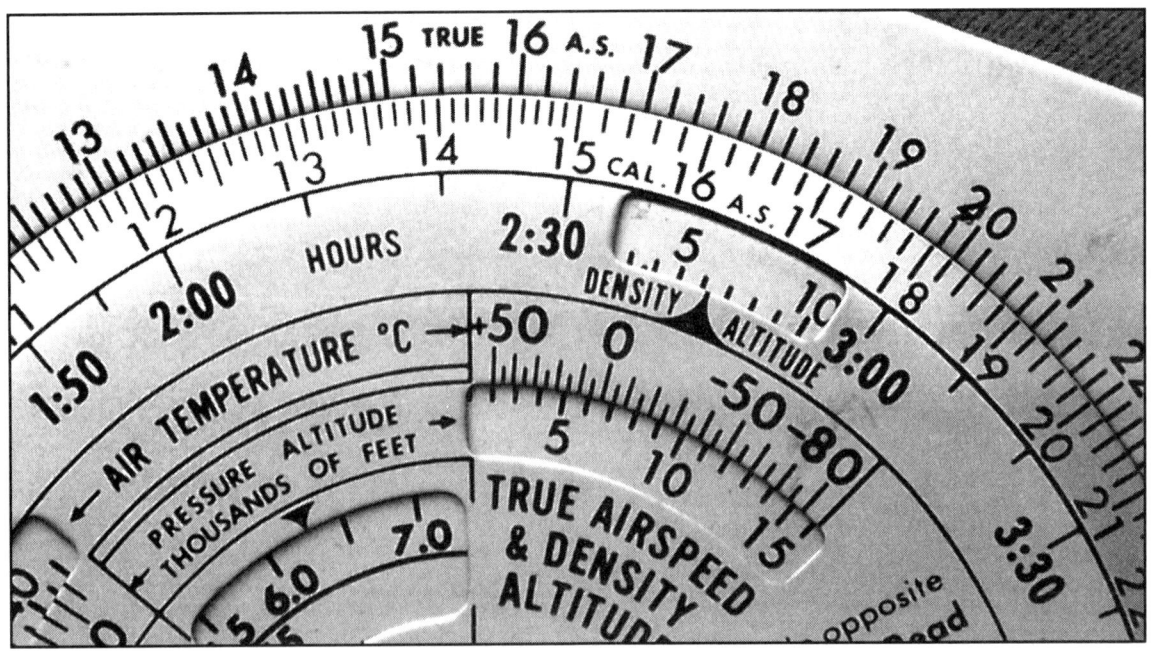

Answer from E-6B: Line up -15C (on Air Temp scale) with 8,000 feet in Pressure Altitude window (right side window). Over 125 on center scale, read 137 on outer scale - that's our TAS.

Real Answer: Not the speed on the Air Speed Indicator. Sometimes, not even close to it.

Remember that our primary interest is ground speed since we are trying to get from "here" to "there". Air speed does not equal ground speed unless there is no wind, and there is practically never no wind.

Headwinds and tailwinds are easy. If the wind is a direct tailwind (fat chance), we add the wind speed to the indicated airspeed to get the ground speed. If the wind is a direct headwind (more likely, alas), we subtract the wind speed from the indicated air speed to get the ground speed. Anything else, and we have to use the E-6B to determine our ground speed (and our heading correction). This is our old friend the wind triangle, which we've done before.

How accurate is your winds aloft forecast? Despite the well-funded and very talented efforts of the weather people, the actual weather does whatever it darn well pleases. Most of the time these forecasts are actually pretty good (and they are getting better), but there will be times when you will be sorely tempted to call up and ask them to confirm that this forecast is in fact for the *third* planet out from the sun. Try to be nice, these people can be really helpful.

How accurate is your air speed indicator? The instrument itself is supposed to be accurate to 2% at low airspeeds, and is allowed to be slightly less accurate, within 8%, at higher speeds. There are, however, quite a few things which affect the accuracy.

Your airplane will have "installation error", which is greater at low speeds than at high speeds. One of the reasons for this is the mounting of the pitot tube. The air speed indicator senses ram air pressure from the pitot tube ("how hard is the wind blowing in?") and compares it to static air pressure. At slow speeds, the angle of attack is such that the pitot tube is pointing upward instead of directly in line with the direction of flight, so the ram air pressure will be affected, and the instrument will read incorrectly.

Air density also affects the indication. As temperature and barometric pressure change, the air density changes, so we get more errors. Some air speed indicators have a correction scale (actually the appropriate scales from a miniature E-6B) on them, or we can figure this correction on our E-6B using outside air temperature, altitude and CAS.

As a rough rule of thumb, we can also add 2% per 1,000 feet MSL to the indicated air speed, but if the temperature is high or low, this will be somewhat incorrect. Using the above example, at 125 KIAS at 8,000 feet, add 16% (or multiply by 1.16) and get 145 KTAS - which conflicts with the answer we got above of 137 KTAS, because the temperature is lower than standard. On a standard day at 8,000 feet, we expect the temperature to be 59 degrees minus 16 degrees (two per thousand feet) or 43 degrees F, which is about +8C. Using the E6-B and changing the OAT to +8C from -15C gives us an answer of 143 KTAS - bingo, it works!

At high air speeds, we encounter compressibility errors. Below 20,000 feet and 200 Knots, we can ignore this because the error is less than one percent. Remember that the vast majority of general aviation aircraft won't go to 20,000 feet or go 200 KIAS, so this really isn't our problem.

For the heavy iron, the correction at 50,000 feet and 500 KIAS is .84, but these guys are probably reading their true air speed off some super-duper big bucks inertial/doppler/GPS sat-nav moving map display anyway, and their biggest concern is "What's it doing now?"

Using the E-6B to plan a flight.

Now that we have all of the bits and pieces, lets put them together and plan a flight.

Our airplane is the mighty BugSmasher 200B. Sleek and powerful, it has a payload of 600 pounds, an empty weight of 1,200 pounds, and a maximum takeoff weight (MTOW) of 1,800 pounds. It can take off in 800 feet (at gross, at sea level on a standard day), and can land in 500 feet (same conditions). It cruises at 110 knots indicated air speed (KIAS), and burns 8.5 gallons of fuel an hour. The fuel capacity is 46 gallons. Best of all, it is paid for.

The flight we are going to plan is a bit more complex than most. We will make a large triangle, stopping twice, and one of the stops will be in Metric-land, where they don't measure things in feet and pounds and inches and gallons. Our last leg will be completed after dark, but that's OK because the airplane isn't afraid of the dark and neither are we.

We have a navigator, too. She weighs 110 pounds and really enjoys flying. She also knows *exactly* what she's doing, having just gotten out of the Air National Guard, and has 1,600 hours in F-16s. Underestimate her competence at your peril.

First thing we do is load the airplane. Our hero pilot (that's you) weighs 170 pounds, our navigator weighs 110 pounds, so that's 280 pounds so far. Payload is 600 pounds, so we have 320 pounds left, which is available for fuel. If we depart with full tanks (46 gallons), that's 276 pounds, so we have 44 pounds left, if we want to use it.

The first leg of our trip is 410 nautical miles. At 110 knots, how long will this take and how much fuel will we need? (We solve for time first, then use the answer to solve the second problem.)

Point the rate index to "11" (speed) on the outside scale. Find 41 (distance) on the outside scale, and read the number on the center (minutes) scale underneath the outer scale's 41 - we see 22.3 on the center scale, but in this case since 11 is really 110, and 41 is really 410, therefore 22.3 is really 223. (We have to remember the decimal location.) It will take us 223 minutes to travel 410 nautical miles at 110 KIAS.

Now look at your wristwatch. Does it go to 223 minutes? Mine doesn't either. So we continue down to the inner (hours) scale and discover that 223 minutes is three hours and 43 minutes. (Use 3 hours 45 minutes and make your life easier.)

(Illustration next page)

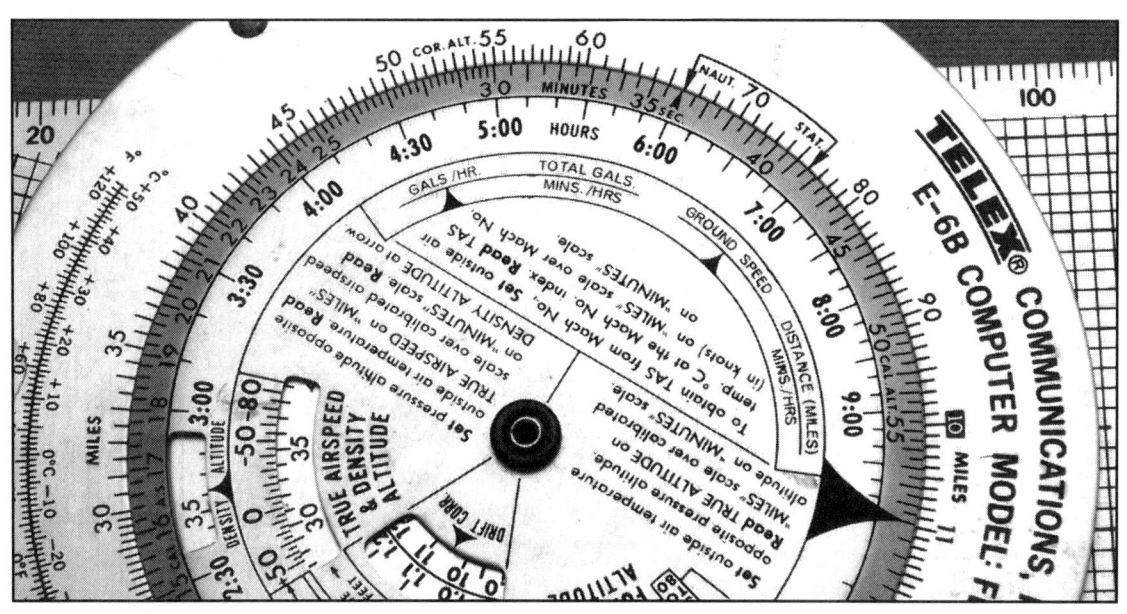

Speed 110 Kts, distance 410 NM, time 223 minutes, or 3 h 43 m

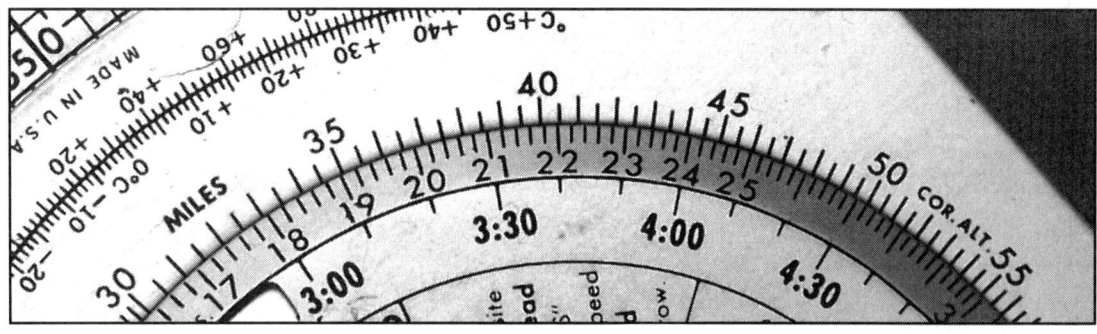

Here's a better look at the 410 NM and the time.

Our BugSmasher burns 8.5 gallons an hour. Do we have enough fuel to do this without stopping AND with a 30 minute reserve as required for daytime VFR flights? Three hours 43 minutes plus the 30 minute reserve is four hours 13 minutes required fuel.

Next, we'll use the rate index as the "fuel use index". Point it to 85 on the outer scale - which is 8.5 gph. Now find 4 hours 13 minutes on the hours scale (hint - use 4 hours 15 minutes, it is easier to find) and read out to the outer scale to determine fuel required with reserves. Answer, 37 gallons. We have 46 of which 44 are usable, so this is no problem.

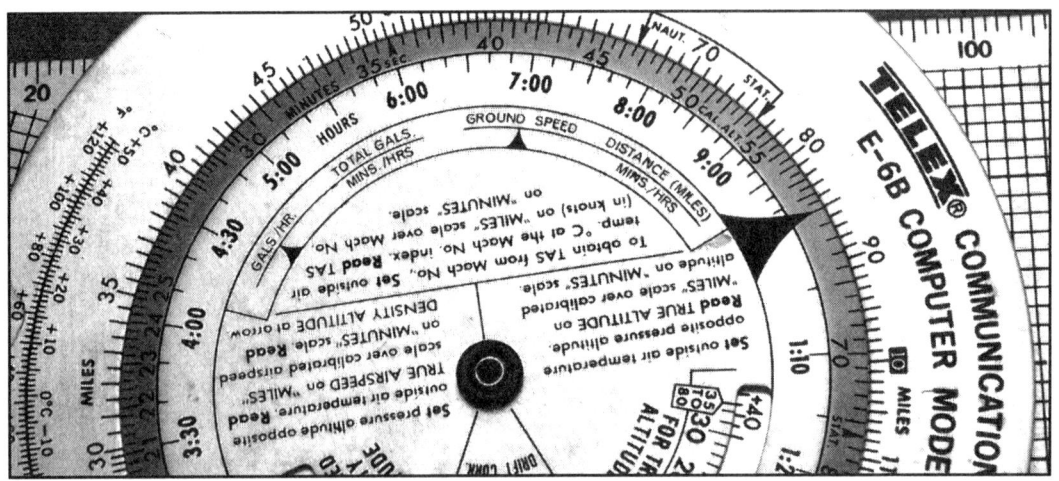

8.5 GPH, 4 h 15 min, read out to 37 gallons required (It is actually 36.5, but I'd rather err on the side of caution here.)

Now we go to the actual flight time of 3 hours 43 minutes, and read out from the hours scale to the outer scale to determine how much fuel we actually will use. Answer, 32 gallons. If we want to know the landing weight of the airplane, subtract the weight of fuel used from the takeoff weight (1,756 pounds takeoff weight minus 32 times 6, or 192, equals 1,564 pounds landing weight.) We will have 14 gallons (84 pounds) of fuel left.

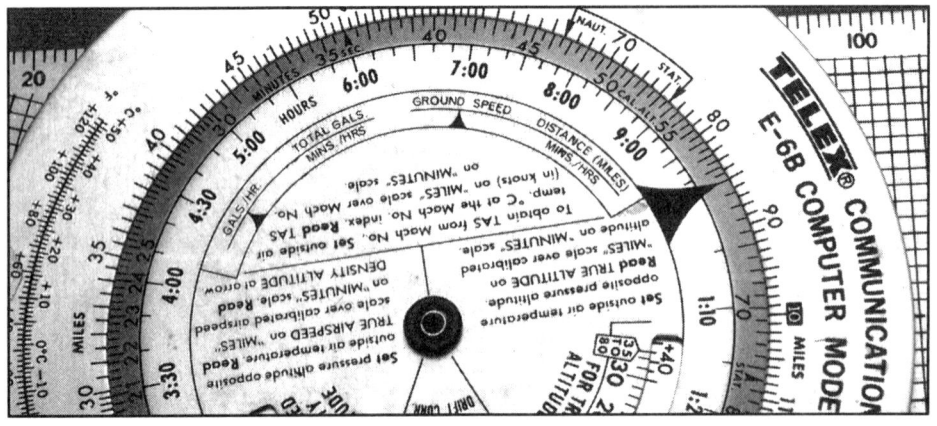

Same picture, this time we are looking for actual fuel required. Read out from 3 h 43 m to 32 gallons.

How do we get the 192 pounds using the E-6B? Line up 32 (US gallons used) on the center scale with the US GAL arrow on the outer scale. Then look at FUEL LBS on the outer scale, and read 19.2 on the center scale, underneath the FUEL LBS arrow on the outer scale. We know that the answer is 192, not 19.2, because we know that the product of 32 times six couldn't possibly be less than 32, so it must be 192.

I've switched E-6Bs here. The 1975 Telex which photographs so nicely doesn't have fuel weight on it, so this is the $11 cardboard special, which does. 32 under "U.S.Gal", 192 shows under "Fuel Lbs."

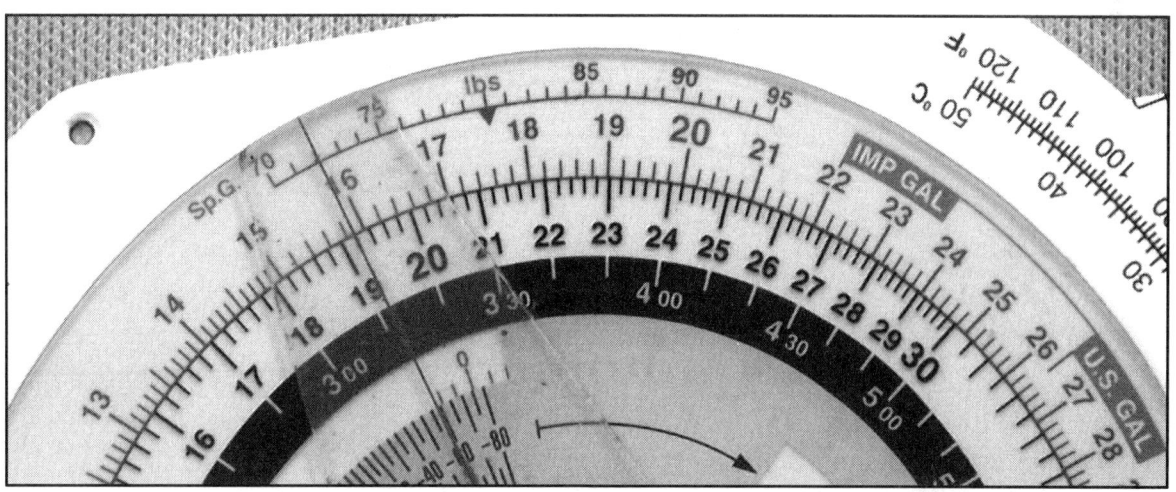

Here's the calculation on the CRP-1. 32 under "U.S.Gal", with the index bar is on .72 on the specific gravity scale. Answer is on the center scale, right around 192 pounds, same as above.

We don't usually figure landing weight on small aircraft, but there are times when it is useful to do so. We will encounter one of those times soon.

Now we know the time in flight and the fuel required to get there, as well as the fuel required to get there with safe reserves. If you have enough fuel to get there but inadequate reserves, change your game plan. Yes, you might make it, but what if the wind changes, or you can't find the airport? Suppose that when you do find the airport, someone is stuck in the exact middle of the only runway, and guess what - you can't land there . . .

We figured the flight in no-wind conditions to give ourselves an idea of the numbers we should be looking for. If we just jumped in and did the wind triangle, and we did it wrong (What? Never happen!), we might not know it was wrong until it was too late.

The problem is that many, many pilots have forgotten how to do wind triangles, and most pilots were never very sure of how to do them in the first place. If you ask a hundred licensed pilots how to do a wind triangle, you'll get 362 different and conflicting answers. Some (not many) of them may be correct. (Yes, I did say that already, but it is still true.)

So lets do the wind triangle for the first leg.

First, we go back to the sectional that we drew our course line on. We take our plotter and determine that our course is 200 degrees true. (True is the line you drew on the map.) Remember that we measured the line to determine that it was 410 nautical miles long. We were careful to use the correct scale (1:500,000, not 1:1,000,000) and we were careful to use nautical miles instead of statute miles.

But if we steer a compass heading of 200 degrees, we are not going to arrive at the airport after 410 nautical miles. We have to make some adjustments.

Adjustment number one is variation. The compass points to magnetic north (somewhere under the snow in northern Canada), and the true course of 200 on the chart is with reference to true north (axis of the earth, the north pole). In the US, the compass error ranges from indicating 20 degrees lower than the actual course in the area of Maine to indicating 20 degrees higher than the actual course in the area of Washington State, with zero error or zero variation (the "agonic line") running more or less from Florida to Chicago.

We look on the sectional and find the magenta dashed lines which indicate variation. They are labeled "5° W", "6° W" and so on. If the letter is E, we subtract the variation from the true course, and if the letter is W, we add the variation to the true course. To remember this, we say "East is least, West is best".

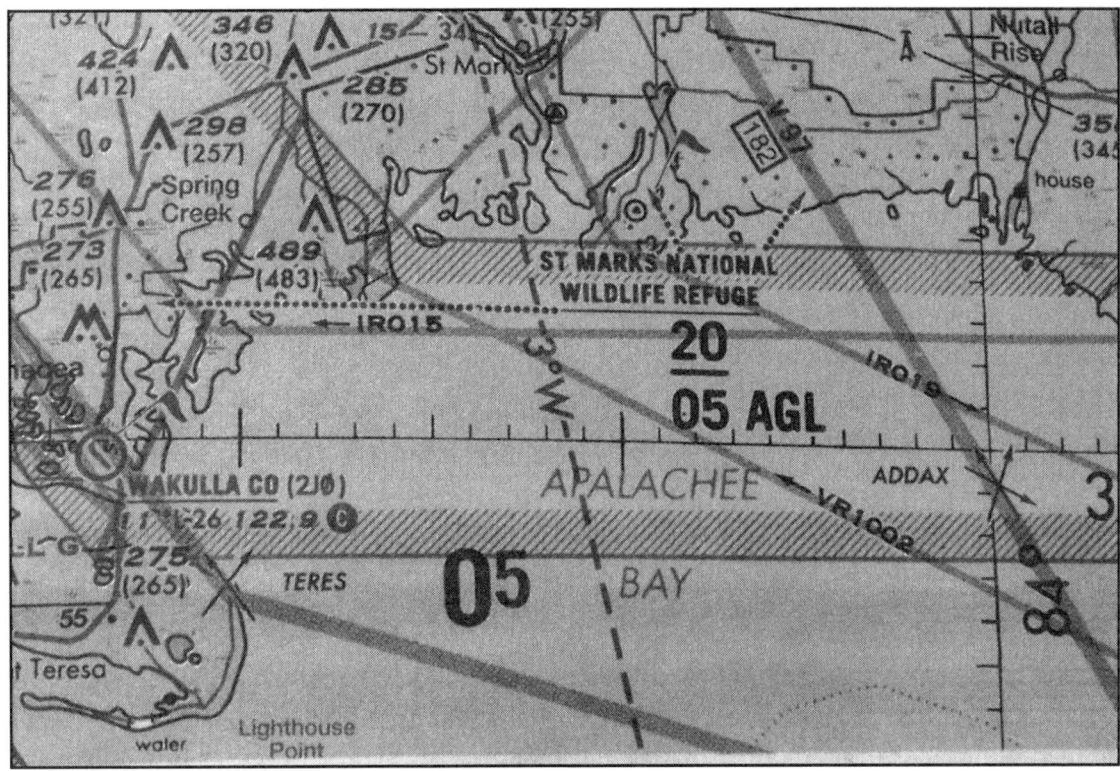

3° W Variation line on a sectional

Here is what is happening: In Maine, if we are actually going 200 (say, by following a road), we will observe that the compass will indicate 220, because the compass reads 20 degrees high here due to variation.

For flight planning: In Maine, where we have Westerly variation, we add the correction factor to the true course to get the magnetic course we want to steer. (West is best). We therefore add 20 degrees to the true course (line on the map) to find the desired compass reading (magnetic heading) to fly the desired course. We want to actually fly 200, so 200 plus 20 equals 220, so we steer an indicated 220, and we are on course, actually flying 200.

In flight: To fly a desired course by compass reference, we would need to subtract the 20 degrees from whatever the compass reads. Since the real course is 20 degrees lower than whatever the compass is indicating, an indication of 220 means we are actually going 200.

In Washington State the compass will read 20 degrees low, so if we fly a known 200 there, our compass will read 180. We have to add 20 degrees to any compass indication to find out which way we are really going.

For flight planning: In Washington State, we have Easterly variation, and we subtract the correction factor from the true course (line on the map) to get the magnetic course. (East is least). 200 minus 20 = 180 (desired compass reading to actually travel 200.)

In flight: If we are reading the compass to determine which way we are going, since we have 20 degrees Easterly variation here, to determine our actual course we would add 20 degrees to whatever the compass says. An indicated 180 plus 20 equals 200, and we are again on course.

(Obviously, all this is a really good way to get lost.)

Trying to remember that we have easterly variation in the west and westerly variation in the east is just too confusing, so we simply look at the sectional and read E or W on the variation lines, and that is that.

We refer to the sectional, and we find that the variation is 10 degrees west where we will be flying. Note that if we fly more or less north-south, we are more or less flying along the lines of variation, and the values will not change much, but if we are flying east-west, we are crossing the variation lines and the values do change. On short flights, take the variation halfway between your origin and destination because you can't read a one or two degree difference on the magnetic compass anyway. On long flights, break them up into a series of short flights and then change the variation for each leg if you need to.

Summary so far: True (the line you drew on the map) plus or minus Variation (where you happen to be) equals Magnetic Course (what the compass should read).

Note One: Our true course in this case is 200. If we decide to come straight home, our true course will be the reciprocal of 200, which is 020. If we are in an area of 10 degrees westerly variation, our compass should indicate 210 on the way out (add for West). Should it read 010 or 030 on the way back?

It should read 030. Variation doesn't care which way you are pointed, only where you are. If you are in Chicago, facing north, New York is to your east and Los Angeles is to your west. If you turn around and face south, New York is still to your east and LA is still to your west. The same goes for true north and magnetic north. They don't change, only your orientation toward them does. If the variation at this particular location is ten degrees westerly, it remains ten degrees westerly no matter which way you turn, or even if you stand on your head (not recommended in an airplane).

Note Two: In the United Kingdom, lines of variation appear on the sectionals in blue instead of magenta, and the variation is called off as 5.5°, 6.5° and so forth instead of whole numbers (5°, 6°) as in the USA. Other than that, they are treated in exactly the same way.

Now we need to go look at the compass card on our BugSmasher 200B. The compass card tells us the deviation error for our individual airplane, and it varies from airplane to airplane and direction to direction. Here is a typical compass card.

For	N	30	60	E	120	150
Steer	360	028	061	090	118	151
For	S	210	240	W	300	330
Steer	180	212	239	270	302	329
DATE						AIRPATH

World's largest compass card. The real item is 1 inch by 1 3/4 inches, or 25 by 43 mm.

This deviation error is caused by magnetic fields in the airplane from the radios, the magnetic effects of various steel parts of the engine, and so forth. If you ever get a chance to install or remove the screws that hold the instruments to the panel, you will notice that they are made of non-magnetic brass. If your passenger puts a portable radio on the glare shield, your compass will promptly point to the magnet in the speaker no matter which way you are going.

In the POH for some aircraft, a deviation error is given with the avionics turned off. For instance, if you turn off the avionics master in a Piper Seminole, the compass promptly swings 20 degrees, because it is no longer affected by the magnetic fields of the equipment it "expects" to feel in normal operation. (Now you not only can't communicate or navigate, you are also going the wrong way . . .)

Since the card calls off the deviation error at the cardinal headings (every 30 degrees), we may have to interpolate slightly. In this case, we want the compass to read 210 degrees (200 true plus 10 westerly variation), and 210 is a cardinal heading. The card says if you want to fly an actual 210, fly an indicated 207. This tells us the compass reads three degrees "low" flying in this direction. If we fly an indicated compass heading of 207 degrees, we will find the airport after three hours and 43 minutes, as long as there is no wind.

Here's how you remember all this:

Your True course is the line you drew on the map.

Variation is where you are, not which way you are pointed.

Your Magnetic course is the true course plus or minus the local variation.

Deviation is specific to YOUR individual airplane, and changes as you change direction.

Compass heading ("steer this way") is your magnetic course plus or minus deviation.

(Note we have not considered wind yet!)

Politically Incorrect Acronym: True Virgins Make Dull Company.

In other words, True +/- Variation = Magnetic +/- Deviation = Compass

Politically Correct Acronym: Tele Vision Makes Dull Company (but no one ever remembers that - wonder why?)

If you ever have to do this backward, it is "Can Ducks Make Vertical Turns?"

We check the weather, and discover that the wind today is 270 at 30 knots.

To do the wind triangle, proceed as follows:

1) Put the wind direction course (270) under the True Index.

2) Move the wind slider card so 100 is under the center hole/metal grommet.

3) Make a PENCIL mark (Ink will NOT come off!!!) at 130.

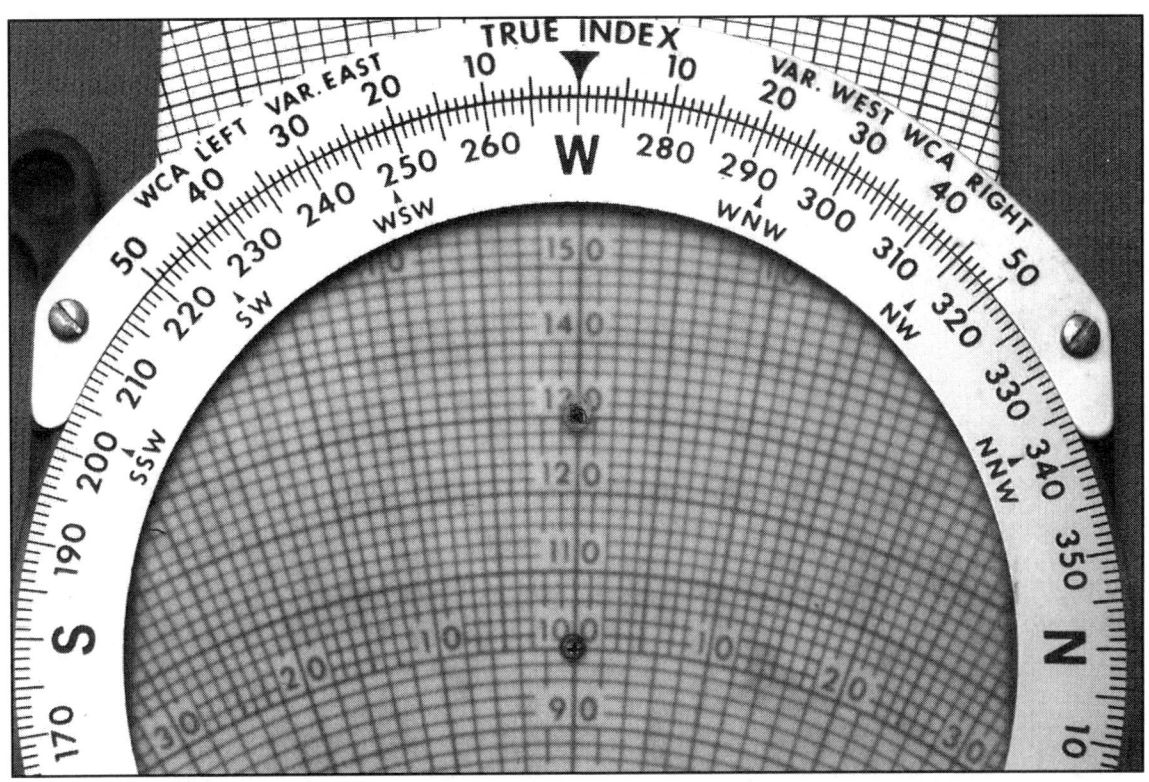

Here are steps 1, 2 and 3. Wind (270) under True Index, center on 100, dot on 130.

4) Turn the wheel so 200 is under the True Index. (Note that the dot has moved to the right and down.)

5) Move the slider card so the indicated air speed (110 for our BugSmasher) is under the dot you made.

6) Examine your results. With the 110 speed arc under the dot, the center hole/metal grommet is on 95. The pencil dot is displaced 15 degrees to the left of the center. This means our new ground speed is 95 knots, and we will have to steer 15 degrees into the wind if we want to track accurately over the ground to our destination. Steering correction is minus if the dot is to the left of the center, and plus if the dot is to the right of the center. If you don't want to remember that, just look which side of the vertical center line the dot is on. Follow the dot - if it is to the right, steer right, if is to the left, steer left.

Compass was 207 degrees, our 15 degree correction is to the left, so we subtract, 207 minus 15 is 192, and that's what we want the compass to read. Whew! So now we know which way to steer to get there.

Our ground speed has dropped to 95 knots, so it is going to take us longer and require more fuel. At 95 knots, the 410 NM will take just under 4 hours 20 minutes, and our time including reserves will be 4 hours 50 minutes.

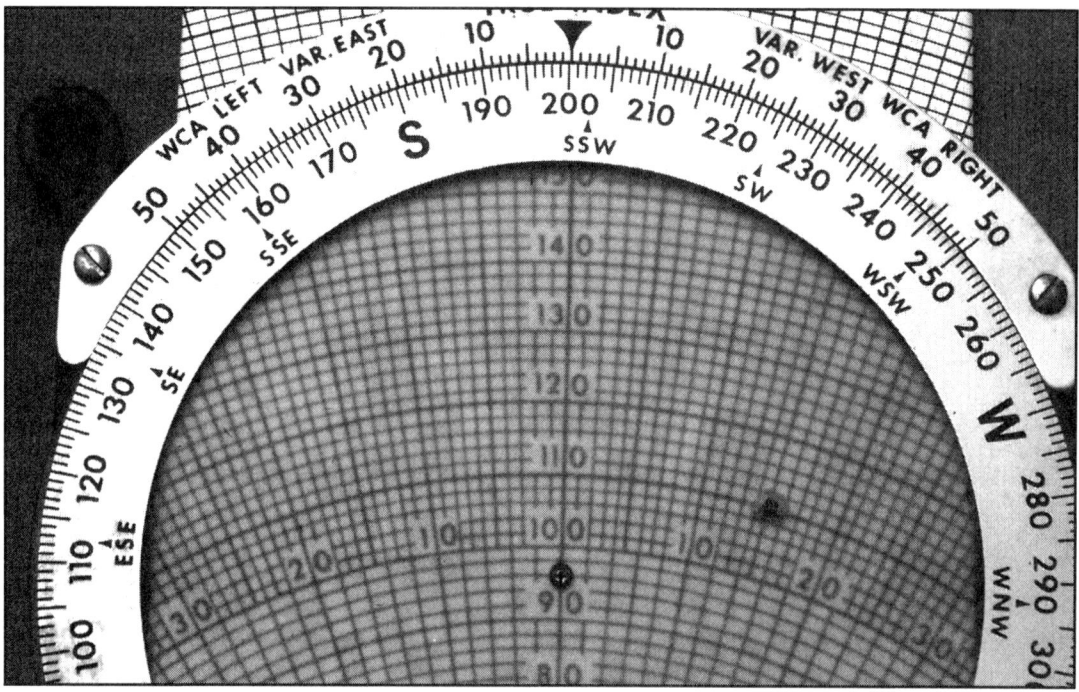

Here are steps 4 and 5, and step 6, which gives the answers. True course (200) under index, 110 under pencil dot, ground speed is 95 knots, wind correction angle is 15° right (add).

To fly 4 hours 20 minutes at 8.5 GPH, we'll need 37 gallons, and the 30 minutes reserve will add another 4.25 gallons to that, so if we don't start with at least 41.25 gallons, we could be in trouble. We are starting with 46 (44 usable), so we are OK, but just - it is starting to get close. In fact, the ultimate range of this airplane is 5 hours 15 minutes from full tanks to "you now have a glider", and I think if there was any more of a headwind, or if this were at night (with 45 minutes reserves needed), it would be a very good idea to make a fuel stop after about three hours. Besides, after three hours, you are probably going to be looking for a bathroom anyway, and that is a good excuse to refuel the airplane as well.

Lets look at the numbers for this flight at night with the same winds. 37 gallons needed, 45 minutes reserves is six more gallons, so we need 42 and we have 46, of which we can only use 44. Those remaining usable two gallons will be gone in just under 15 minutes. Are you comfortable with that? I'm not. Remember that winds aloft do have a habit of changing, and airports have a habit of hiding themselves better and better as your fuel runs lower and lower.

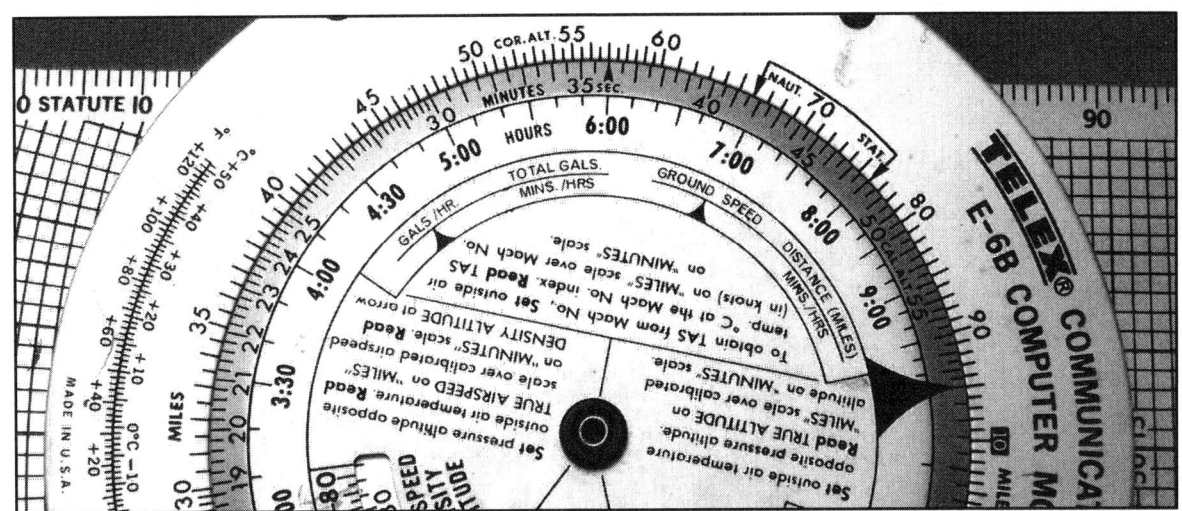

Final time calculations: At 95 knots ground speed, 410 NM will take us 4h 20 m, so at 8.5 GPH, we need 37 gallons plus 4.25 reserve during the day, or 37 plus 6 at night which is 42 gallons of the 46 gallons usable, and that's too close, thank you.

Summary:

Draw a line on the sectional between where you are starting from and where you are going.

Measure the line to find the distance. Use your plotter to determine the true course.

Do the True Virgins Make Dull Company sequence to determine the compass heading you would steer if there was no wind.

Figure the time required and the fuel required in no-wind conditions. Remember the required fuel reserves are 30 minutes daytime, 45 minutes at night.

Check the weather for the winds aloft.

Do the wind triangle to determine your new ground speed, which determines your new time en route and your new fuel required (remember reserves). Compare to fuel available, remembering unusable fuel!

Determine the wind correction angle and add or subtract it to the compass heading to determine which direction you will actually steer to get there.

With a little practice, this whole sequence takes perhaps five to ten minutes, tops.

You should do this even if you plan to make this flight navigating by pilotage, by IFR (I follow roads), by VOR, by ADF (my, are you brave) or by GPS, because none of these will tell you that you are about to run out of fuel. You do NOT want your navigator asking you why it suddenly got real quiet in here. Doing the wind triangle is the only way to know how long this flight will really take, and unless your BugSmasher is the model with air-to-air refueling capability, fuel management is vitally important. In fact, one of the top three ways pilots manage to get themselves killed is by simply running out of fuel.

Reality check: We figure our flight time based on distance and speed. While distance doesn't change, if we climb to altitude, the speed does. Remember that we get a 2% increase in airspeed for every 1,000 feet of altitude, therefore if we make this flight at 6,000 feet, we are going to get an increase of 12% over what the air speed indicator says, even though it is reading precisely 110 knots. Our actual air speed is therefore 110 + 13.2 knots, or 123.2 knots. This means under no-wind conditions, the 410 nautical miles will take us 3 hours 30 minutes instead of 3 hours 45 minutes, and we'll need just under 30 gallons of fuel instead of 32 gallons.

Since there is almost never "no wind", the change in our airspeed changes our wind triangle results. Our ground speed will be slightly higher, and our wind correction angle will be slightly less. This is why choosing checkpoints along the route is a good idea. No matter what else changes, if you fly toward something you can see, you will get where you are going.

These are not huge differences, but you should be aware of them and the reasons they arise. It quickly becomes obvious that planning for and carrying adequate reserve fuel is an extremely good idea. There are many variables in the actual flight which we cannot plan for. The wind may change, the temperature may change, ATC might want us at 4,000 or 8,000 feet for a while (which affects the free 2% per 1,000 feet increase in airspeed), the airplane might be slightly mis-rigged and burn a bit more than the stated 8.5 GPH, the tachometer may be wrong, so we are actually at 72% power or 78% power instead of 75%, we might not be paying attention and find ourselves somewhat off course, and so on. Strive for accuracy, but don't be totally upset if the results don't exactly match your calculations.

Now take a break. You have absolutely earned it.

Welcome to Metric-land

Four hours and twenty minutes later, the airport in Metric-land draws into sight. Hurrah, we need a rest.

When we did our original flight plan, we noticed that according to the Metric-land sectional, the length of the runway was shown as "1,000" and it is at 1,300 meters MSL. 1,000 is an awfully short field for our BugSmasher. Even though we can get it on the ground and stopped in 500 feet, we need 800 feet to take off again, and that is at sea level. That 1,000 is going to be tight.

Actually, there's not a problem. Our navigator took the E-6B and found the arrow for feet on the outer scale and the arrow for meters on the center scale, then lined them up. The runway length is given in meters, not feet, and 1,000 meters (on the center scale) converts very nicely to 3,275 feet (on the outer scale), which is ample for us. The elevation of 1,300 meters MSL converts to 4,250 feet, so pattern altitude is an indicated 5,250 feet or thereabouts.

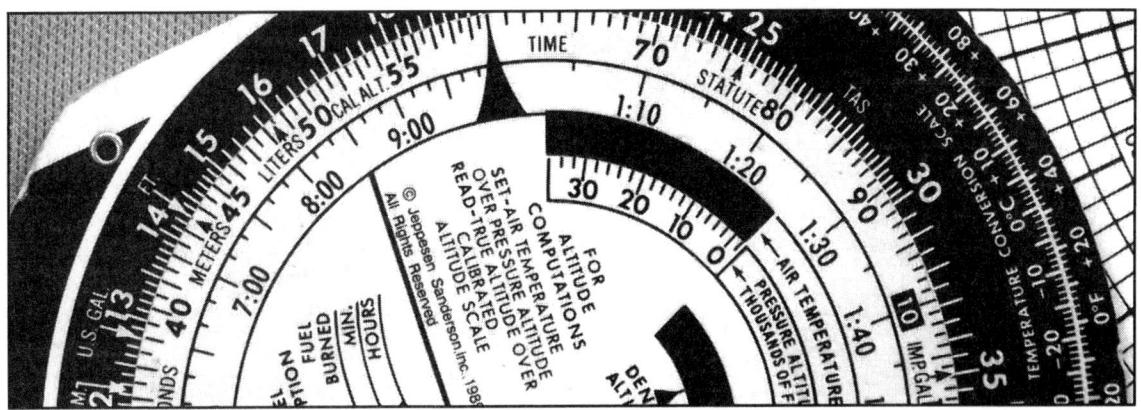

Feet and Meters arrows lined up on the left, 1,000 meters under 3,275 feet on right. The airport elevation conversion of 1,300 meters to 4,250 feet is done the same way.

As we approach, we talk to the tower, since we need to know the active runway and the local barometric pressure. We are told the local barometer is "1013.25 millibars". Well guess what - there is no conversion on the E-6B for millibars to inches of Mercury, or reverse, so we have to call the tower again and ask them for the barometer in inches, please. We are told that it is 29.92 inches.

In the United Kingdom, when we ask this question, we may get a response like "QFE is 992" or "QNH is 1016". These "Q" codes are left over from WW2 when airplane radios mostly used Morse code. After all, when people are shooting at you, you would tend to be terse. Just about everything you can imagine had a "Q" code, and most of them are now long gone.

QNH is the equivalent of the US "altimeter setting is", and if set to this number, you will have your height above MSL. QFE is the altimeter setting which will produce a reading of "0" when you are on the ground at the airfield, which may or may not be at sea level.

While this does make figuring the pattern altitude easier (the altimeter now indicates the height above the ground), I am not sure that having your head down and locked fiddling with an altimeter while you try to enter the crowded traffic pattern is a real good idea. Our UK friends seem to have it worked out, however, so I'll shut up about it now.

If you do a lot of flying in Metric-land, you might want to photocopy the following conversion chart and tape or glue it to the high speed side of the wind slider. The high speed side goes up to 650 knots (or 650 mph, if you are working in statute miles), and there is no way our BugSmasher will ever go that fast, ever.

inches	millibars	inches	millibars	inches	millibars	inches	millibars
26	880	28.25	957	29.5	999	30.5	1033
26.5	897	28.5	965	29.75	1007	30.75	1041
27	914	28.75	973	**29.92**	**1013.25**	31	1050
27.5	931	29	982	30	1016	31.5	1066
28	948	29.25	990	30.25	1024	32	1083

While you do have permission to photocopy this chart, this specifically does not give permission to photocopy the rest of this book. It is protected by copyright, and if someone sees it and wants a copy (and they will), being a nice guy and making a photocopy of your book will start some serious trouble with Uncle Sam. They will have to buy their own. Sorry.

It is a hot day today, and the outside air temperature is 90 degrees. The airport is at 4,250 feet MSL, so we are hot and high. We are also going to be heavy, because we have a long flight ahead of us (take a lot of fuel), and we are picking up a present for Grandma (more about her later) which weighs 53 kilograms. We can just fit the present into the back of the airplane, but we are going to have to calculate our weight and balance carefully.

First, lets figure the density altitude because we need to estimate our takeoff run and climb performance. The empirical method ("Let 'er rip, we'll see if we can make it!") is not conducive to long life and happiness. If the performance of the airplane is going to be inadequate, we want to know *before* we try it, not after.

While the outside air temperature gauge on our BugSmasher is calibrated in Fahrenheit, the weather people (if we can talk to them in Metric-land) will give us the temperature in Centigrade. The E-6B needs the temperature in Centigrade to calculate density altitude correctly. This is easy, we simply look at the bottom of the flight computer and find that 90 degrees F is equal to 32 degrees C.

Now we go to the density altitude windows. The double window is where we input our information, and the single window is where we find the answer, the density altitude. We find +32 C in the top, and line it up with a little over 4 in the window. We have to look carefully, because the numbers are very small, and the graduations are smaller.

Now we look at the actual density altitude - it is close to 7,000 feet! While our BugSmasher 200B performs well at sea level, since it isn't turbocharged, the performance falls off the higher we go. According to the POH (Pilot's Operating Handbook, which we know better than to seriously believe), at sea level we find we can climb 850 feet per minute on a standard day, but at a density altitude of 7,000 feet, our rate of climb drops to 420 feet a minute! We also discover we need 1,400 feet of runway at 7,000 feet, as opposed to 800 feet at sea level.

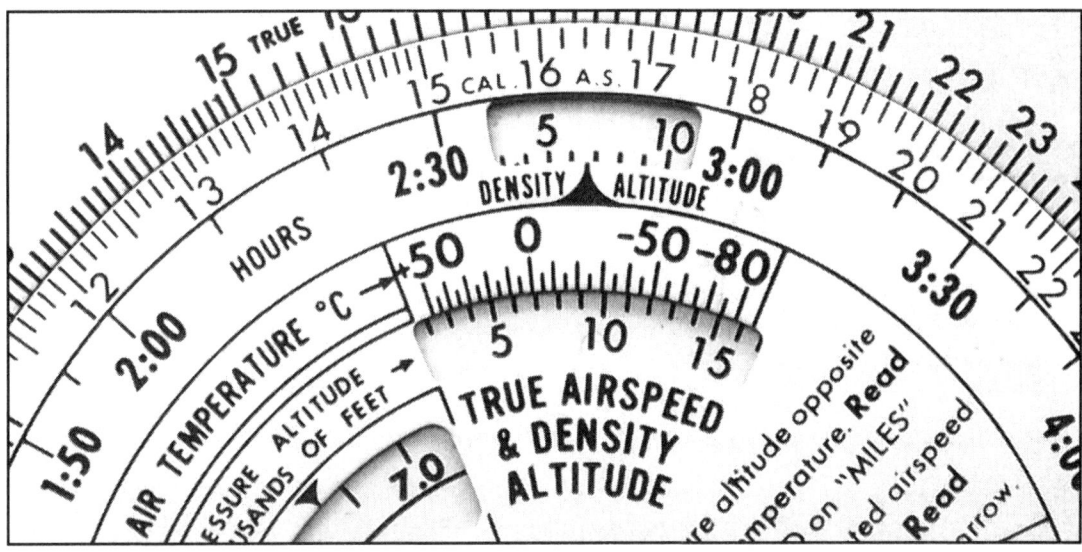

Air temperature (+32°C) over 4,000 feet MSL in lower window, read density altitude in upper window. It shows a bit more than 6,500 feet, and we will round it up for safety's sake.

Here is the loading manifest for our return flight:

Pilot:	170 lbs	170 so far
Navigator:	110 lbs	280 so far
Cargo:	53 kgs	?
Fuel:	unknown	?
================		
Total:	600 lbs payload	

We have a 600 pound payload available, and you and your navigator make up 280 of it. We are also loading that 53 kilogram box into the airplane, so next we need to know what 53 kg is in pounds.

This is an easy conversion. Find the Lbs arrow on the outer scale and the Kg arrow on the middle scale, and line them up. (Look carefully.) We discover that 53 kg is 116 pounds! Try not to tear the upholstery as you muscle the box in and tie it down securely.

Lbs over Kg on the left side   **53 under 116 on the right side**

Now it looks like this:

Pilot:	170 lbs	170 so far
Navigator:	110 lbs	280 so far
Cargo:	116 lbs	396 so far
Fuel:	unknown	?
================		
Total:	600 lbs payload	

Add 116 to the 280 we already have, and our total is 396, before we add the first drop of fuel. Lets call it 400 to make our lives a little easier.

600 minus 400 means we have only 200 pounds of available payload left now, and we do need to fuel the airplane. Find the FUEL LBS arrow on the outer scale and put 20 on the center scale underneath it. Now find the US GAL arrow on the outer scale, and read 33.25 underneath it on the center scale. Fine, we can put 33 gallons of fuel into the airplane and still be at or just below MTOW.

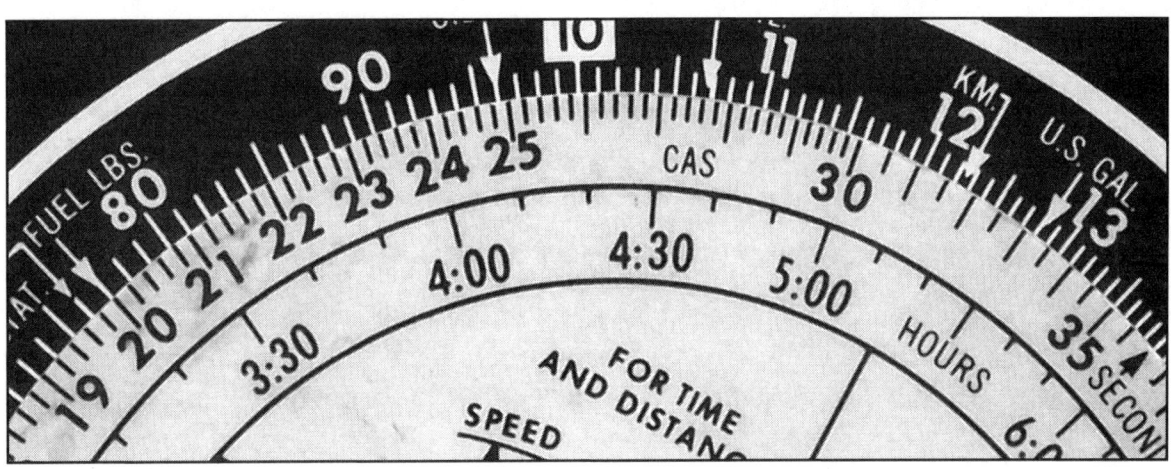

200 under Fuel Lbs, that's a bit over 33 US Gallons.

But we have two problems. Problem number one is that we don't know precisely how much fuel is already in the tanks (the fuel we didn't burn in getting here), so we can't know what it weighs, and problem number two is that the fuel pump here in Metric-land isn't calibrated in gallons, but is instead calibrated in liters.

We can approximate the answer to problem number one by figuring out our fuel consumption from our departure point, remembering we left with full fuel, or 46 gallons. In four hours 20 minutes at 8.5 gallons an hour, we've burned 37, so it makes sense that we have about nine gallons left. This is a good approximation, but if the fuel consumption is a little less or a little more than we expected, the actual amount of fuel on board will not be the nine gallons we expect. Furthermore, not all of those nine gallons are usable. (Check the POH for "unusable fuel". It is exactly two gallons on the BugSmasher.)

You should be aware that aircraft fuel gauges are notoriously inaccurate (they are evidently made by the same people who make Ouija boards, and work almost as well), and in fact the only place where the FAA requires them to read correctly is when they read "empty". I already know I am out of fuel, thank you very much. Spit. Pop. Sputter.

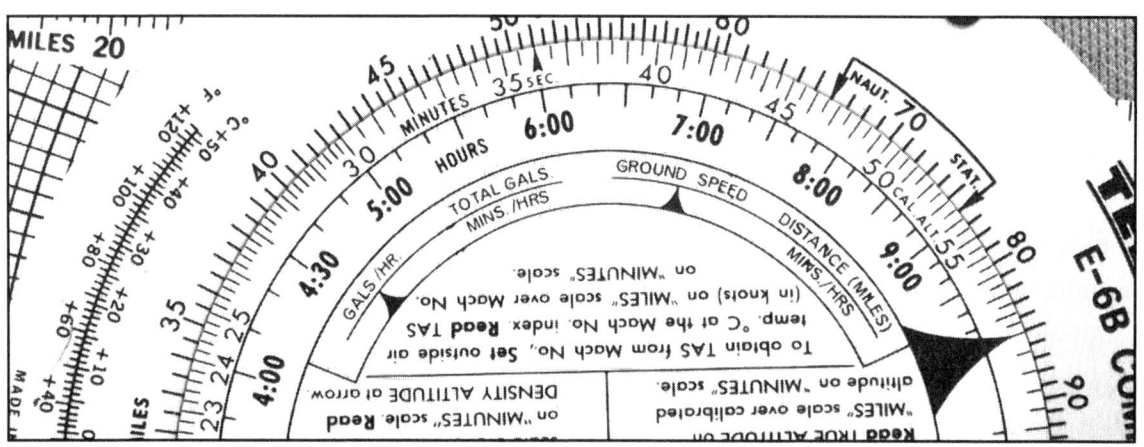

Here is 4 hours 20 minutes at 8.5 GPH, about 37 gallons.

The best way to find out is to "stick the tanks" with a calibrated dip stick. These are available for most light aircraft and are inexpensive and a very good investment. Make sure you get the correct dip stick for YOUR airplane because the same model of aircraft may have different fuel capacities depending on year or options. (And try not to accidentally drop one into the fuel tank, it is extremely embarrassing to be seen fiddling around for half an hour trying to fish it out again.) We discover we actually do have nine gallons in the tanks, so now we know we have 54 pounds of fuel already on board. The total we can carry is 200, so we can add 146 more pounds of fuel (24.25 gallons), and we will be right at MTOW.

Our final manifest looks like this:

Pilot:	170 lbs	170 so far
Navigator:	110 lbs	280 so far
Cargo:	116 lbs	396 so far
Fuel:	54 lbs +146 lbs	596 to here, better stop now.
====================		====================
Total:	600 lbs payload	Four pounds left. Eat a light lunch.

Here is why we need to do this - If we tell the line boy to "fill it up", we'd have 13 extra gallons, or 78 extra pounds of fuel in the airplane, and our takeoff weight would be 1,878 pounds, which is over MTOW.

These extra 78 pounds could result in a bent airplane, (on this departure we are hot, high and heavy), and I guarantee you that after the crunch, the very first thing the FAA and the insurance company will do is figure a weight and balance, and you better be under MTOW and within CG, or else! If you blissfully went ahead filled the tanks and then added a third person and his suitcase (which is probably full of rocks), well, your career in aviation is not showing a lot of long-term promise. MTOW means MTOW, and triply so if we are hot, high and heavy.

Now we need to convert 24.25 gallons to liters, so we can tell the line boy how much fuel to put into our airplane. Find US GAL on the outer scale, and put 24.25 under it on the center scale. Find LITERS on the outer scale, and read how many liters are equivalent to 24.25 gallons - and the answer is 92 liters, please.

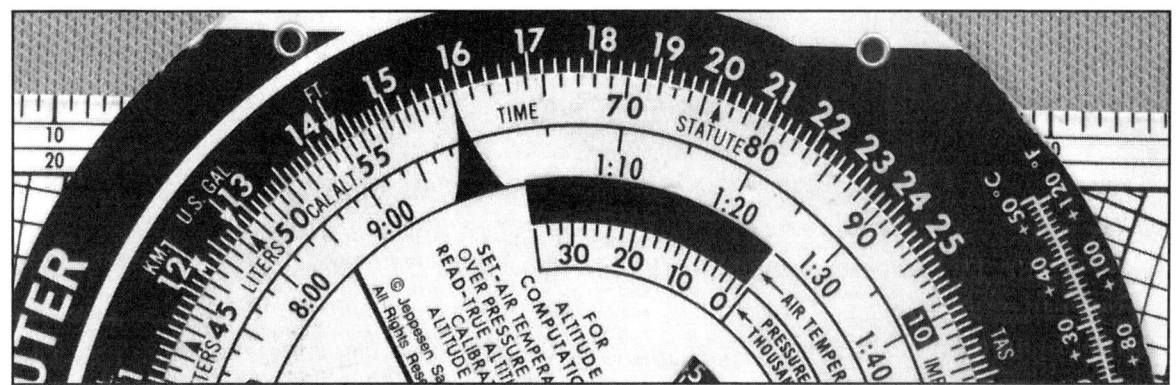

US Gal arrow over Liters arrow (look carefully, it is on the left), 24.25 gallons equals 92 liters (and you read that on the right).

Same conversion on the ARC-1. 24.25 under US Gal, index bar on Liters, read 92 on center scale.

We are now good to go as far as MTOW is concerned, but we also need to figure out if we have enough fuel to get home without stopping somewhere on the way for more.

Fuel on board:	33 gallons
Minus unusable fuel:	2 gallons
Minus reserves (30 mins)	4 gallons
==============	========
Total usable fuel:	27 gallons

At a fuel burn of 8.5 gallons per hour, 27 gallons gives us an endurance of three hours 10 minutes, which at 110 knots gives us a range of 345 nautical miles. That's in still air, and you will notice that it is less than the distance to go home. If the time home is 3 hours 45 minutes (which was our no-wind time out), we would need to use 32 of the 33 gallons of fuel on board. Remembering we can't use the last two, this not only leaves us no reserve at all, but we also can expect the engine to sputter to a stop seven minutes short of where we want to touch down. This just isn't going to work.

Your navigator will be extremely annoyed at you if she ruins her nylons and her expensive Manolo Blahnik shoes struggling out of the woods to get help for you in your wrecked airplane, which you ran out of fuel just a few miles (13, to be exact) short of your destination. It could be even worse if the wind changed.

You will also notice that it is getting late, and the latter part of this flight will be done at night. This means you will need 45 minutes reserve fuel instead of 30, or about 6 gallons instead of 4. Therefore, you have only 25 gallons of fuel before you are into the reserves, and that 25 gallons gives you an endurance of three hours twelve minutes. At 110 knots, that is 325 nautical miles, which is 85 miles short of home.

Does all this sound like it might be a good idea to stop for fuel somewhere? You're absolutely correct! And remember, we have not even figured the wind triangle yet, so it could easily be much worse.

Fortunately, we are not going home yet, so all this worry is for naught. Remember this trip has a stop on the return leg, so we are not going to have to fret over not having enough fuel to get home from Metric-land because we are not going directly back anyway.

Metric-land to Grandma's Airport

Our next stop once we leave Metric-land is Grandma's Airport. While this sounds like an odd name for an airport, that's really what it is. Grandma has always been an aviation enthusiast, and when she sold her dot-com business last year for eighty six gazillion dollars, the first thing she did was to go out and buy her very own airport. With all that money, she did it right: 6,500 feet long, 350 MSL, an on-field VOR, ILS and VASI, avgas and jet A, and a fleet of silver Audi A4 convertibles as courtesy cars.

Grandma's Airport is 250 NM on a heading of 055° from Metric-land. At 110 KIAS, in still air, we'll take 2 hours 16 minutes, and at 8.5 GPH, we'll need 19.4 gallons of fuel.

110 KIAS, 250 NM, answer 2 hours 16 minutes

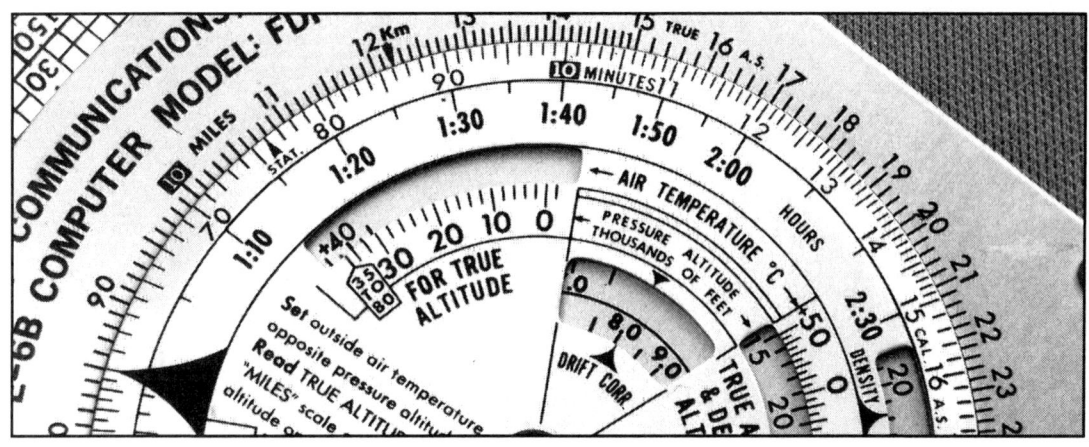

8.5 GPH, 2 hours 16 minutes, answer 19.4 gallons

The wind today is 270 at 30, unchanged from earlier. Doing the wind triangle, we find that our new ground speed is 132 knots!

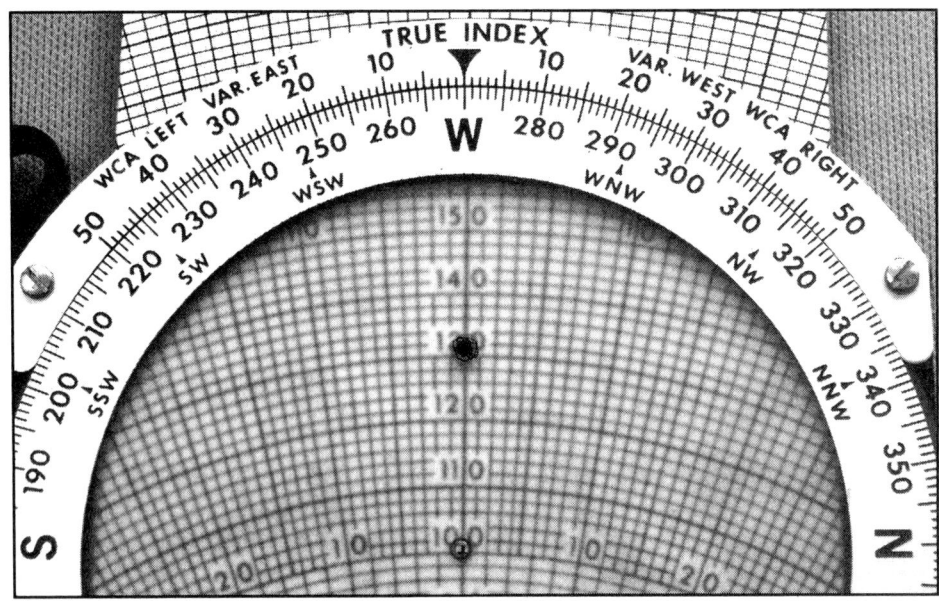

Step one for wind triangle: Wind direction under True Index, center on 100, dot up from center at wind speed (thus 130, remember we are using 100 as zero).

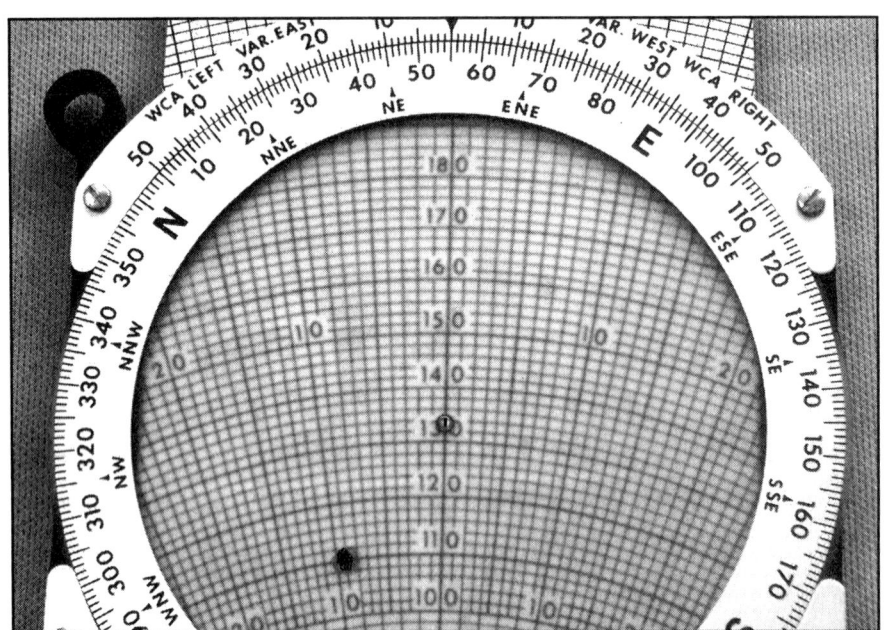

Step two for wind triangle: True course under True Index, the dot has moved left and (way) down, move slider card to place 110 (the indicated air speed) under dot, answers are 132 Knots ground speed (under center), 9° correction angle to the left, under the dot.

This means the 250 nautical mile trip will take us only one hour 55 minutes and require only 16.5 gallons of fuel. Yes, tailwinds are wonderful - when you get them. Variation is still 10 degrees west, so we add 10 to the heading of 055 to get 065. The deviation card says that to fly a heading of 060, steer 058, so we subtract 2 degrees, we will steer 063. Finally, the wind correction angle figures out to be -9°, so we would steer an indicated 054° to get there.

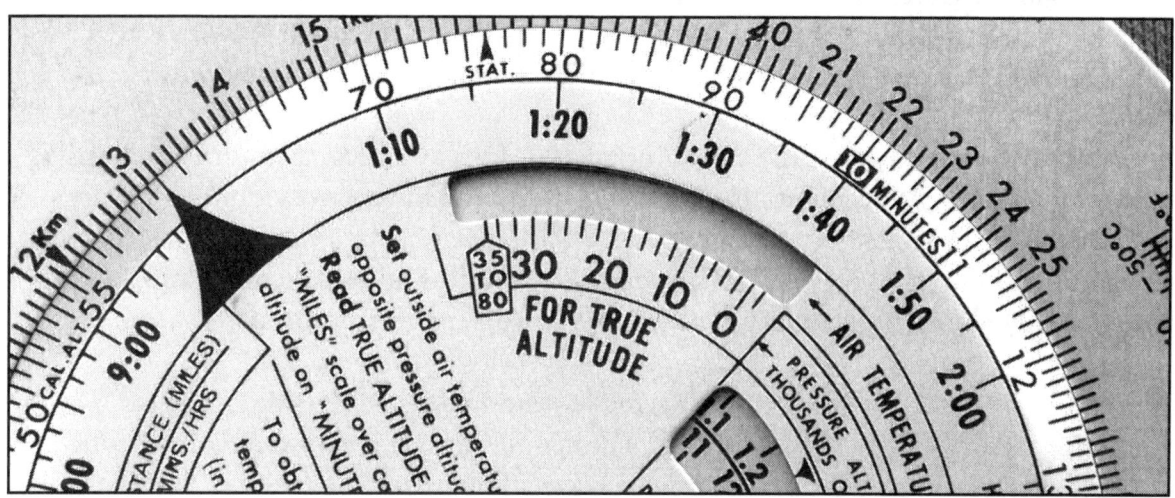

Our new ground speed of 132 Knots gives us a time of 1 hour 55 minutes for the 250 NM to our destination.

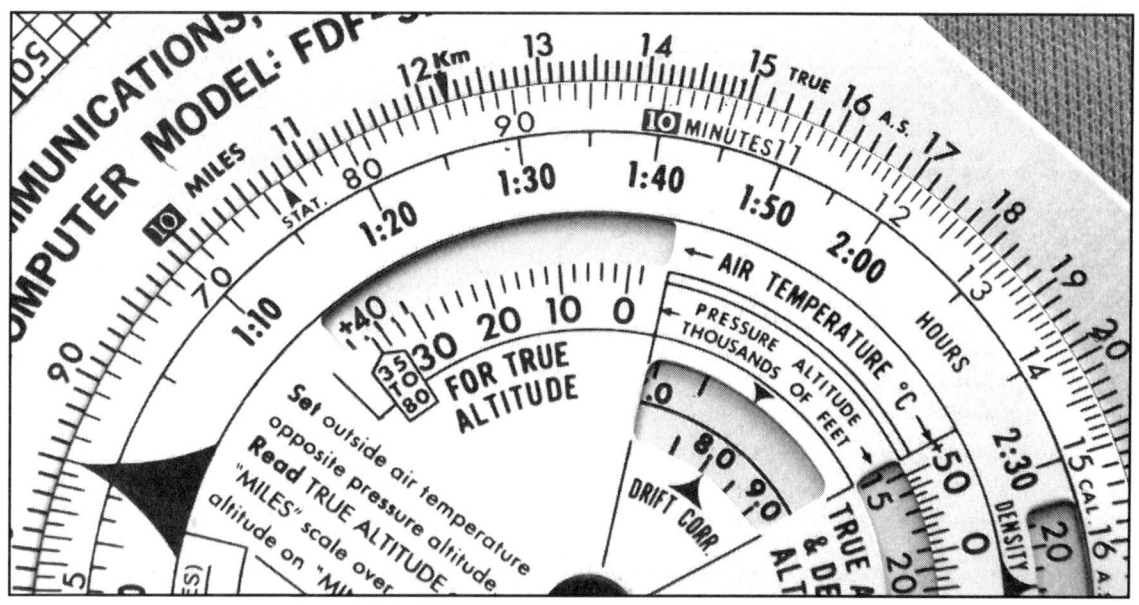

Our new time of 1 hour 55 minutes means we will need 16.2 gallons at 8.5 GPH.

Looking at the sectional, we discover that if we follow a true course of 055°, we will fly exactly through the middle of a Military Operations Area ("MOA"). Normally, this isn't a problem, but the name of this particular MOA is "Ka-Boom Lake Nuclear Test Range", and while it is not listed as active at the time of our flight, we would prefer not to discover first-hand that the information on the sectional is wrong. Furthermore, if we have engine problems and have to make an emergency landing and wait a couple of hours to be rescued, our future progeny (if there are any) may have two heads and glow in the dark. We are well advised, in the interests of good airmanship, to detour around this evil place, and we will.

Our detour will be as follows: Fly a heading of 100° for 150 miles, then turn to a heading of 020° for an additional 175 miles. The way we got these numbers was simple. We drew our detour on the sectional, then measured the distances with our ruler, and determined the course lines with our plotter. We will be going 325 nautical miles instead of 250, but this 75 nautical mile detour will keep us out of trouble if we need to stop for any reason.

Our checkpoint for the turn is a large, perfectly round lake just outside of the MOA which suspiciously resembles a very large crater, but the military claims it was like that when they got there, so it must just be a coincidence. The local name for the lake is "Smoking Crater Lake", but that must be simply another odd coincidence.

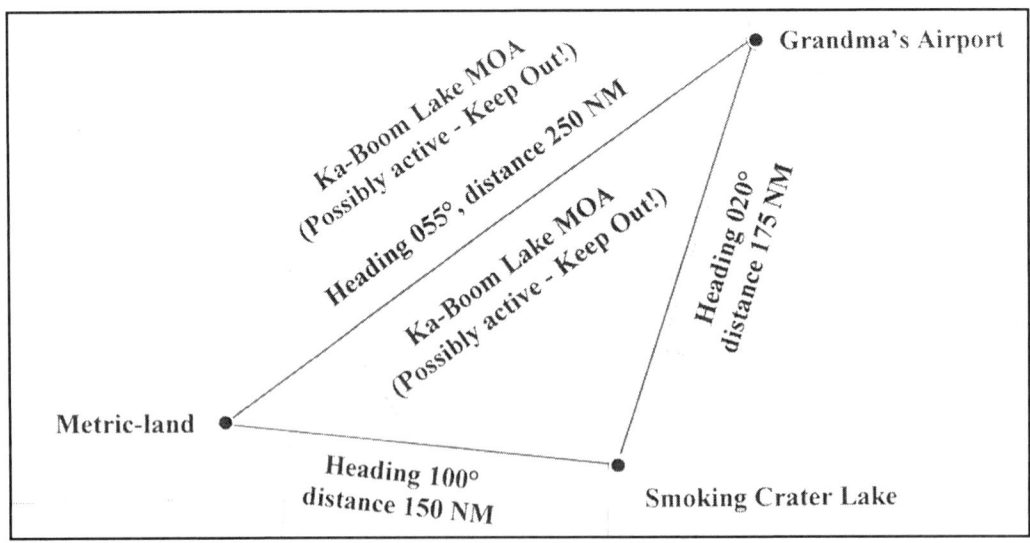

Not for navigation. This page probably intentionally not blank. Absolute accuracy guaranteed for ten feet or ten seconds, whichever comes first.

The wind is still 270 at 30, and doing the wind triangles gives us a very respectable ground speed of 140 knots on the first leg, which means it will only take us 1 hour 5 minutes to cover the first leg, then when we turn to our 020 heading, the wind gives us a 115 knot ground speed, and the last 175 NM will take us one hour 33 minutes. Total time is thus 2 hours 38 minutes (call it 2 hours 40 minutes), total fuel is just under 23 gallons. This means for the price of 43 extra minutes in the air and 6 gallons of fuel, we have avoided the dangers of a forced landing in the middle of the MOA and becoming unwilling extras in some grade B mutant radioactive zombies from hell movie. That's a good tradeoff in my book. (Wait a minute, this *is* my book. Never mind.)

This 23 gallons of fuel will weigh 138 pounds. If we add half an hour reserve fuel, or 4.25 gallons, that's another 25.5 pounds, so we need to have a minimum of 27.25 gallons, or 164 pounds of fuel for the flight. Guess what - we have 200 pounds of fuel in the tanks already (33.3 gallons), which as you recall brought us to MTOW.

Here is our fuel management:

We have 33.3 gallons on board
less 2 gallons unusable
less 4.25 gallons more for half an hour reserve
gives 27 gallons available, which at 8.5 gallons an hour is a touch over 3 hours 10 minutes, which at 110 KIAS in still air is 340 miles.

This should make you smile since we calculated the flight from Metric-land to Grandma's Airport even with the detour at 2 hours 40 minutes and needing only 23 gallons of the 27 we have available.

Now lets refine our figures: Metric-land to turn is 150 NM, true course is 100, variation is 10W, deviation card says 120/118 so the error on a heading of 100 is going to be about -2°.

True: 100
Var: +10
Mag: 110
Dev: -2
Compass should read 118 (if no wind)

Wind correction angle is 3 degrees right, so we steer 121. Ground speed is a whopping 140 knots. Time enroute (from takeoff to turn point of 150 NM) is 1 hour 5 minutes, which requires 9.2 gallons of fuel.

At the turn point to Grandma's airport, distance remaining is 175 NM, true course is 020, variation is 10W, compass card says 360/001 and 030/033, so we'll figure the deviation at +2° on this heading.

True: 020
Var: +10
Mag: 030
Dev: +2
Compass should read 032 (if no wind)

Wind correction angle is -15 (left), so we steer 017, Ground speed is 115 knots, so time enroute is 1 hour 33 minutes, fuel required is 13 gallons.

Total time is 2 hours 38 minutes, total fuel is 22.2 gallons.

One last check of the density altitude (no change), a final preflight, and off we go.

Flight line at Grandma's School of Aviation

Grandma's Airport to Home.

The last leg of our journey is from Grandma's Airport to home. The distance is 250 nautical miles, and the heading is 345°. At 110 knots and 8.5 GPH, this means 2 hours 15 minutes and 19 gallons of fuel. Unfortunately, the wind today is not kind to us and has shifted to 360 at 20, almost a direct headwind. Our ground speed will drop to a disappointing 90 knots, which means the trip will take 2 hours 50 minutes, and require 24 gallons of fuel.

We've also been flying almost seven hours today already (4:20 to Metric-land plus 2:32 more to Grandma's Airport), and this is getting to be a LONG day. Besides, Grandma has graciously offered us the use of one of her modest 12 bedroom nine bath guest villas, with two pools, three Jacuzzis and a widescreen HDTV in each room, and heck, who are we to refuse this hospitality?

We are up bright and early next morning and ready to depart for home. For this last leg, however, you are going to be on your own, as I have decided to stay and enjoy Grandma's hospitality a few more days (or maybe weeks).

You already know the distance is 250 nautical miles, and the true course is 345°. The rest you are going to have to figure out for yourself.

1) Distance is 250 NM, air speed is 110 knots, how long will this take if there is no wind?

2) Once you have the time, at 8.5 GPH, how much fuel do you need (also no wind)?

3) True is 345°, variation is 12W, compass card says 330/333 and 360/001, so interpolate the deviation and do TVMDC to determine the compass heading (again, before wind).

4) Check wind: It is 090@20 today.

5) On wind triangle side, determine new ground speed and determine drift angle.

6) Using new ground speed, figure new time in flight.

7) Using new time in flight, determine fuel required.

8) Add/Subtract (and you tell me which) wind correction angle to compass to determine correct compass reading to get us home.

9) Calculate fuel remaining in airplane on arrival at Grandma's, add fuel required to get home, add fuel required for reserves. Compare with MTOW. Since we are rid of that heavy box, we may be able to depart with full fuel - this is worth calculating, since as you know, the only time an airplane has too much fuel in it is when it is on fire. (Or if we are hot, high and heavy.)

Write your answers here:

1) time in flight, no wind

2) fuel required, no wind

3) compass heading (after TVMDC)

4) new ground speed

5) new time required

6) new fuel required

7) new fuel required plus reserves

8) correct compass reading to get us home

9) gross weight at takeoff

I'll help you with this last one. MTOW is 1,800 lbs, empty weight is 1,200 lbs, payload is 600 lbs. You and your navigator/co-pilot weigh 280 lbs together, leaving 320 lbs for everything else. You're not taking anything else home, so you can use all 320 lbs for fuel. If you filled the tanks to 46 gallons, that's only 276 lbs of the allowable 320 lbs, so go ahead and top off the airplane. You don't really need to know how much fuel you had when you arrived at Grandma's (it was 12.1 gallons, by the way) since you are filling it up, and that is a known quantity. You'll still have 44 lbs left for all that "Souvenir of Grandma's Airport" junk you bought in her gift shop - and the soft, fluffy logo towels that somehow wound up in your RON ("remain overnight") kits.

Answers:

1) time in flight, no wind is 2:17, so call it 2:20 to make our lives easier (and longer - always assume you'll need MORE fuel rather than less. Better to land with a gallon too much than a gallon too little.)

2) fuel required, no wind is 20 gallons.

3) compass heading (after TVMDC) 345° + 12° +2° (or so) is 359°.

4) new ground speed is 114 knots

5) new time required is 2:12

6) new fuel required is 18.5 gallons

7) new fuel required plus 30 minutes daytime VFR reserves is 18.5 + 4.25, or 22.75 gallons

8) correct compass reading to get us home with a wind correction angle of 10° to the right is 009°.

9) gross weight at takeoff is 1,756 lbs, since we decided to fill it up and didn't buy anything in the gift shop. We are good to go.

That's all there is to it. It really wasn't all that difficult, and as you see, Phil Dalton's little invention is going to be around for a long time to come because it really, really works well.

Understanding Variation

The compass error known as variation is caused by the 1,300 to 1,400 mile difference between the location of true north, which is the north pole, and magnetic north, which is in Labrador, Canada.

The variation error does not change with the direction we are going. It remains constant, and it depends only on where we are. Example: If I stand in a field in Pennsylvania facing north, New York is to the east of me and Chicago is to the west of me. If I turn around and face south, New York is still to the east of me and Chicago is still to the west of me.

The compass needle tries to align itself with the earth's magnetic field, so the north end wants to point to the north magnetic pole, and the south end wants to point to the south magnetic pole.

In Maine, magnetic north is to the west of true north, so the "north" end of the compass needle is pulled toward the west ("westerly variation"), and the compass card will rotate slightly counterclockwise. The result is that no matter which way we are pointing while we are in Maine, the compass will indicate about twenty degrees higher than our actual direction.

Sitting on the ground doing our flight plan, we add twenty degrees (add for westerly variation) to the direction we desire (the line on the map, our true course), and this gives us the indication we want to see on the compass. To go 070 true, steer 090. To go 340 true, steer 360. To go 160 true, steer 180.

In flight, subtract twenty degrees from whatever the compass says and that's the direction we're really going. Compass says 090, we're going 070 true. Compass says 360, we're going 340 true. Compass says 180, we're going 160 true.

In Washington State, the north magnetic pole is to the east of us. Here, the "north" end of the compass needle is pulled toward the east ("easterly variation"), and the compass card rotates slightly clockwise. No matter which direction we fly, the compass indicates 20 degrees lower (less) than our actual direction.

For flight planning, subtracting twenty degrees from the direction we desire (the line on the map, our true course) gives you the indication we want to see on the compass. To go 090 true, steer 070. To go 360 true, steer 340. To go 180 true, steer 160.

In flight, add twenty degrees to whatever the compass says and that's the direction we're really going. Compass says 070, we're going 090 true. Compass says 340, we're going 360 true. Compass says 160, we're going 180 true.

Now lets apply this to flight planning.

We first draw a line on the map between where we are and where we want to be, and then we use our plotter to determine the TRUE course. (True is the line you drew on the map.) Our true course for A to B in Maine turns out to be 070. Co-incidentally, our true course for the trip from C to D in Washington State also is 070.

Now we determine the local variation, and if it is east we subtract it from true to get magnetic, if it is west, we add it to true to get magnetic. The mnemonic is "East is least, west is best." That means if we are in a area of easterly variation, we subtract the variation from the true course to get the magnetic course, and if we are in an area of westerly variation, we add the variation to the true course to get the magnetic course.

For our Maine trip from A to B, true was 070, the local variation is 20°W, so we add 20 to 070, therefore the desired compass reading will be 090. Steering an indicated 090 takes us over the ground on an actual course of 070. (West is best, add.)

For our Washington State trip from C to D, true was 070, the local variation is 20°E, so we subtract 20 from 070, therefore the desired compass reading will be 050. Steering an indicated 050 takes us over the ground on an actual course of 070. (East is least, subtract.)

That's all there is to it, and now you know why.

(A note on variation: If you look at a sectional, you will see that the variation lines seem to be smooth, regular arcs. This is a typical case of "the map is not the territory". Variation sometimes differs from the map value due to slight disturbances to the earth's magnetic field, such as from deposits of iron ore under the surface. These errors do tend to be localized, but they tell us that placing ultimate and absolute faith in the precise compass reading may not be a wonderful idea.)

Final Comments

1) The POH (Pilot's Operating Handbook) for some older airplanes is often a thin little booklet which seldom says more than "The pointy end is the front." Performance figures are frequently optimistic in the extreme, and seemingly written by the sales department.

Newer airplanes (from about the mid 1970s) have better, more complete manuals, but it is still a poor idea to place your ultimate faith in what the book says the airplane will do. Remember that the airplane isn't new any more, and quite possibly couldn't match the book numbers even when it was.

2) When navigating by pilotage (as in "look out the window"), hold the sectional to match the terrain. We like to read maps with north at the top since the words are upright that way. If we are heading north and holding the map with north at the top, the map will match the terrain. Heading south but still holding the map with north at the top means the map is upside-down in relation to the terrain, and you will be *so* lost *so* quickly it will amaze you.

Be sure you have current sectionals. Airport frequencies change, there are constant changes to where you can and can't (or maybe don't want to) fly, and new and ever taller TV towers sprout like weeds. Using outdated sectionals is both illegal and dangerous. If your GPS has an updatable database, be sure it is current. All this information (printed sectionals or bytes on a chip) is only current as of date of publication, so just because the map says there's nothing to run into, you still need to look outside - something new may have just been built.

3) If you look at the magnetic compass and see a little row of air bubbles at the top of the window, it is time for a rebuild. There's a rubber diaphragm under the back cover, and after a few years it gets hard and starts to crack and leak. Refilling the compass (use Stoddard solvent, a thin kerosene) just postpones the inevitable, and not by much.

You can only read the compass in straight and level un-accelerated flight. Turns, turbulence, changes in airspeed (and probably evil spirits) all affect the indication. Let the compass settle down before you confidently announce "our heading is XXX degrees!"

4) Go out and have a good time. Take pleasure in doing everything you do as well as you can, and never stop learning. Aviation is an obsession for which I hope there is no cure.

Best Regards,

Mike Arman, AGI